KU-621-204

What's Your Vibe?

Leabharlanna Chathair Bhaile Átha Cliath
Dublin City Libraries

What's Your Vibe?

TUNING INTO YOUR BEST LIFE

CRAIG DAVID

EBURY
PRESS

1

Ebury Press an imprint of Ebury Publishing,
20 Vauxhall Bridge Road,
London SW1V 2SA

Ebury Press is part of the Penguin Random House group of companies
whose addresses can be found at global.penguinrandomhouse.com

Copyright © BTDI LTD 2022
Cover photograph © Rankin 2022

Cover design by Kieron Lewis | kieronlewis.com

BTDI LTD has asserted its right to be identified as the author of this
Work in accordance with the Copyright, Designs and Patents Act 1988

First published by Ebury Press in 2022

www.penguin.co.uk

A CIP catalogue record for this book is available from the British Library

ISBN 978-1-52910-972-6

Typeset in ITC Galliard Pro by seagulls.net
Printed and bound in Great Britain by Clays Ltd, Elcograf S.p.A.

The authorised representative in the EEA is Penguin Random House Ireland,
Morrison Chambers, 32 Nassau Street, Dublin D02 YH68

Penguin Random House is committed to a sustainable future for
our business, our readers and our planet. This book is made
from Forest Stewardship Council® certified paper.

*This is for all of you who have
been with me for the last 22 years,
and for all of you who are just tuning in.*

CONTENTS

Here With Me

How are you feeling? Are you happy? Calm? On top of things? At one with the world? If so, stop reading for a moment and close your eyes. Tune in. Take a deep breath and, as you breathe out, just feel how nice it is to be in this vibration – those are good vibes.

Maybe, though, the answer isn't so straightforward and you aren't feeling calm or at one with things. Maybe something's a bit 'off'. Maybe you feel an external niggle, like an arrangement you made that later you'd rather not be a part of, or a wave of uncertainty, or something has left you feeling edgy or anxious. Or perhaps those moments when you're calm and happy and life is smooth have become few and far between.

If any of these scenarios chime with you, then chances are that you're out of balance and you may need to do some realigning to get back into the flow of your good vibes.

When I'm out of flow and feeling disconnected from my good vibes, life gets hard. I can feel mentally, and physically, drained and spiritually empty ... like all the drum beats, basslines and harmonies that've been keeping me tuned and alive to the world, connected and excited and wide-eyed, have stopped and the music is silenced.

I've been there many times, but I've come out the other side again. While my sense of balance can still be a bit off from time to time, what I've learned is that if I'm connected to what makes me feel alive mentally, physically and spiritually, then I feel more optimistic, clear and purposeful. And instead of putting off my joy to some future event, I'm more present and happy in this moment.

•

Over the last 22 years, through all the beautiful times and through all the wonky times, I have met success, I've met failure; I've met adulation, I've met humiliation; I've been chubby, I've been at peak fitness; I've been surrounded by people, yet at the same time deeply lonely; I've been riding the crest of the wave, but inside crashing down to the bottom of the sea.

And through all of this, my vibes have been uber-positive. I've been the one with the biggest smile, the one with the can-do attitude, the one who always wants to make it nice for everyone around me. If you had a problem, you could always count on me to spin the most optimistic, most positive answer, to put

I've learned that there is a different way to be.

myself out as far as I could go to solve it – even if I was walking on shaky ground or the solution came at great cost to me.

But, over the past few years – since an injury caused me to re-evaluate everything that I'd held to be true; since allowing myself time to learn, to reflect, to open my eyes to what's around me – I've learned that there is a different way to be. That reframing negative situations or uncomfortable moments as positive, was, at times, a mechanism to avoid going deeper. That sometimes moments *aren't* positive and, however you want to reframe them, it's important to sit with the truth for a moment and, within that, as you relinquish control, there's profound wisdom. *That's* the reframing, because you are honouring the actual situation rather than sweeping the discomfort under the carpet.

I am now in a place where I can be true to myself, but it hasn't always been this way. This is not a traditional memoir, and it's not a self-help book either. Instead, it's a series of lessons learned from a life lived, many of which I've only real-ised in retrospect – after all, it is only through living that we can learn and grow.

I, in no way, have all the answers – I'm still learning, still making mistakes, but I feel ready now – after a lot of twists and turns along the way – to share my journey with you.

This, then, is my story of how I have learned to tune into my best life.

CHAPTER ONE
Thief in the Night

Up until 22 March 2018, my positive vibes were so dazzling they'd have blinded you. Being positive was in my blood, coursing through my veins. I was the guy who, however he was feeling on the inside, always said yes; always brought the good vibes to the party; was always up for it, a boundless, frenetic ball of optimism. I was feeling creative, confident and bold, open to new opportunities and new collaborations, and the music – what I loved – was flowing. But this all changed one chilly New York morning at the ABC studios, just as I was about to go on *Good Morning America* to perform my latest single 'I Know You', when those vibes came crashing down so hard, the lights went out.

Something was off the night before in the hotel gym, when I'd felt this niggle in my back – something I hadn't felt before and put down to all the travelling and lack of sleep in between performances. With an early start the following morning and my obsessive adherence to my training, I hadn't had time to think about it until I was alone in my dressing room. My vibes were wonky. Not because this was a live gig in front of millions of people, syndicated across the US, or because this was a big deal – for me, for my team, a lot was at stake. It was because these nervy pains were now radiating down my back and, even though I was doing stretches, my hands down on the floor, legs extended, I wasn't getting any relief. The constant coming and going of studio staff, in and out of my room – 'is there anything we can get you?'; 'sign this form'; 'make-up will be ready for you in ten'; 'sound check in twenty' – was making me feel anxious and super-triggered. Ironically, on the TV in my dressing room, a couple were talking about the drug they were taking for their back pain, the same back pain apparently felt by millions of Americans, and all I could think was: *whatever it is, load me up*.

My vibes
were wonky.

Knowing that I had 15 more minutes to try to decompress my back, I was becoming more and more anxious. As I lay on the floor trying one last attempt to ease my back nerves, there was another knock at the door that was so loud it felt as though the whole door was about to come off its hinges. I was met by a frantic studio runner who had come to tell me that it was my last call and to make my way to the stage. Jumping up (which, by the way, was *not* a good idea), I rushed along a tight corridor, a stone's throw away from the raised stage I was about to perform on, and was told to hold there for a moment while my in-ear monitors were placed over my head and a microphone put in my hand. I felt overwhelmed by the frantic movements of the studio crew, people shouting instructions to one another and then, suddenly, I heard, 'Craig, you're on in one minute; you need to get into position …'

Taking my first step onto the stage, I felt this razor-sharp pain, a bolt of agony so severe that I'll never be able to wipe the memory of it. It was like that nerve pain you get if the anaesthetic isn't working while your tooth is being drilled – searing and paralysing at the same time. I could feel myself grimacing, ready to fall, but as I caught sight of the musicians already on set, their smiles gleaming, their excitement at being live on *Good Morning America* jumping out at me, it was enough for me to shut down the noise my body was making and release the adrenalin that allowed my legs to take a second step up onto the stage. I told myself to focus on the stage manager's countdown and three–two–one, I locked myself in. As the show's host approached to introduce me, I dug down deep and pulled out my biggest beam. Whatever else was going on, I had my vocals and, as America watched and people back home tuned in, I sang and I smiled and I vibed … and, all the while, my back spasmed. When I finished my set with 'Magic', the audience cheered and it was over.

It was over, but, for me, it was only just beginning. A few moments later, standing in front of the huge digital billboard in Times Square – to this day I'm still not sure how I physically made it out of the TV studio – with my album cover, *The Time Is Now*, glowing like a halo over me, all I could think of was that now, *right now*, I was on a countdown before my face would crack and my smile dissolve into tears.

NOTHING LIKE THIS

Back at my apartment in Miami, my descent into hell took a dive into the deep dark blue. Whatever the doctors, physios or specialists tried to do – injections, medication, physical therapy, the works – something had happened that no one had the answer to. There was nothing that could stop the pain and spasms for more than a few hours at a time and, even in those short bursts of relief, knowing that the pain would blindside me at any time, from any angle, got in the way of everything.

There was the physicality of it – sharp, jagged stabs that left me ragged and exhausted – and then there was the constant, draining emotional intensity of it.

Deep down, I felt that reaching out about my turmoil was the highest form of weakness. That giving away the power of fixing things myself was giving in, big time. You see, for so long, I thought that being hard and strong, being physically robust, would protect me. But now my body was broken and, for the first time in my life, I could feel myself hurtling downwards.

With no immediate way out and no foreseeable solution to the physical pain, I spiralled. I didn't want to get up, I didn't want to go out. I didn't want to see anyone and I couldn't motivate myself to do even the smallest of tasks. The worst thing was not being able to sleep – those endless, unforgiving nights when I couldn't even toss and turn such was the pain. I just lay there, desperate to get comfortable. Lying there in agony, all these dark thoughts would come to the surface and, even if I closed my eyes, they were still there. Morning would come and there would be no relief and I knew I couldn't go on like this. It was like my Pandora's Box opened and, as the lid came up, I went down. For the first time in my life, shocked as I admitted it to myself, I was depressed.

Depressed. A word, a state of mind I'd previously never even thought about. But now I was beginning to understand that it's as real and as true as anyone can say real or true. I came to see that all the less than positive things I'd been burying and not confronting about my life had started to snap me in half. And let me tell you, that was not easy to face. I got to a point when I thought that life wasn't worth living, that I would be happier if I wasn't here anymore. If this was my life, then I would have to dip out.

I can't tell you how much this shook me up. I'd wake up from maybe an hour's sleep all night, lying in agony, and think: this can't be me; this can't be my life. I'm the Iron Man. The Happy Man. The I-Can-Do-Anything Man. Mr Positive. Nothing could touch me.

But I knew. I knew that this absolutely was me and it absolutely was my life and that I had to do something about it …

If this was
my life, then
I would have
to dip out.

CHAPTER TWO
The Story Goes ...

Looking back at my childhood, one thing is for sure, I was happy – cared for and loved by my parents and grandparents. Even though my parents divorced when I was eight and I lived with my mum, I saw my dad on weekends and they made the split as smooth as they could for me. I was very close to my mum and my nan, both of whom were always there for me and giving in so many ways that I felt secure. While we had little money, living off my mum's wages from her job in TM Stores (Southampton's equivalent to Superdrug) and living in a small council flat on the St Mary's estate, this meant that I was able to throw myself into my passion for music.

From a very early age, I was intrigued by the little hi-fi set-up and big box of records in our living room. At home, we'd listen to music all the time – my mum and dad's vinyls were the soundtrack to my life, and I'd join in with Terence

Trent D'Arby, Stevie Wonder or some old-school reggae artists like Garnett Silk or Beres Hammond, without even realising I was singing. Sometimes I'd make up my own lyrics, freestyling over the top of the track. My dad was the bass guitarist in a roots revival reggae band called Ebony Rockers. Not only did I love their grooves and melodies, but I always felt moved by their lyrics. Their strong message of fighting against social injustice and racism, which they had all experienced in their lives, somehow hit me in my soul, even if I didn't understand it all at that age. Knowing that my dad had played a part in creating this made me proud and there was nothing better than pulling out his records, excited that there he was on the front cover – yes, my dad. He and I listened to endless hours of different reggae hits, from volume 1 all the way through to about volume 100. There were so many of them, and every week it seemed that a new one came out.

My dad was a huge influence on my musical education. His love of music had come from his childhood in Grenada, where he'd grown up before coming to the UK. He gently encouraged me to take guitar lessons and, because my hands were 'big enough', I was able to start early. However, after giving it a go, I wasn't really feeling it. The lessons took place in a musty, cramped attic and the whole classical vibe wasn't for me back then. My dad was cool with that. Music should never be forced. It needs to flow from the outside in and then from the inside out, and he could see that my rhythm and my passion lay elsewhere.

The first record I ever bought was a 7" edition of Michael Jackson's 'Human Nature' and, from then on, vinyls became *everything* to me. It felt a small miracle that I could put them on this inanimate object, place a needle on top and music would play out, filling my soul. I loved organising and arranging things, having been a keen stamp collector with the encouragement of my grandmother's brother, Uncle David. He'd taught me all about classifying and arranging stamps in albums – he had original Penny Blacks in *mint* condition that we'd gaze at adoringly – and I loved the care and precision it took to place them in my album, that chalky white paper crinkling over the top of my newest stamp. So, when it came to records, I was already a bit of a pro at the art of collecting.

I loved the thrill of watching the charts and looking out for new releases. I guess you could say I was on the obsessive side – poring over the back pages of my precious magazine *Touch*, which kept me up to date with what was going on with R&B music in the UK and hip-hop in the US; and *Blues & Soul* that listed all the new releases that were coming out over here and all the ones that were going to be on import from America. Best of all was the list of what was 'on promo' – not yet officially released, but likely to be available through specialist record shops or played by some DJs. We didn't have a record shop that stocked R&B or hip-hop in Southampton, but we did have Movement which fast became my local go-to store for jungle and drum and bass, which I also loved.

As soon as I was allowed to go to the high street by myself, I'd put on my best clothes and, with a spring in my step, head to Movement. I'd savour the moment, standing in the doorway, inhaling the crispy incense, before taking a deep breath of happiness, walking in, making my request – mostly tracks I'd identified from the back of my magazines – and waiting for the music to start. I'll always remember hearing Shy FX's remix of Ray Keith's 'Chopper' for the first time – the flood of the beat and bass through the huge speakers was the biggest thrill. Every time I stood by those speakers, listening to new music, I'd think, *life can't get much better than this.*

If I'd saved enough pocket money or had some spare cash from doing odd jobs, I'd buy a record, and I can still remember the electric anticipation as, back home in my bedroom, I'd rub the wrapping on my jeans so I could pinch a bit of cellophane and tear it open, inhale the fresh vinyl smell, lower it onto the deck, put the needle down and then ... the listening. Taking it all in, feeling the beat course through me, was a moment of true happiness.

The first gig I ever went to was with my mum to see Terence Trent D'Arby at Southampton's Guildhall. We had front-row seats so I could see everything. The whole experience blew my mind – the band, the sound and watching him perform. He was moving like Prince with a bit of Marvin Gaye in his step, but

Taking it all in,
feeling the beat
course through me,
was a moment of
true happiness.

he had a voice like Stevie Wonder with a bit of Michael Jackson thrown in. When he sang his huge breakout hit 'Sign Your Name', I wanted to sing with music signed across my heart, and I went home with something shifted inside me forever.

WHEN THE BASSLINE DROPS

By the time I was off to secondary school, my record collection was growing beautifully, inspiring me to start writing my own lyrics. I didn't yet have any of my own music, so I'd use the instrumentals on the B-side of my records, my dreams coming true as I sang over the music of some of my favourite producers: Dr Dre's beats, Rodney Jerkins' tunes. I'd spend hours and hours in my bedroom ad-libbing, introducing them, just like the DJs I listened to on the radio.

It's probably true to say that I was obsessed with music. I knew the names of every producer, I knew where the snare was taken from one track and where the kick drum was sampled from another; I knew when the bass hit, I knew when my heart was touched by a lyric. I was *in* it.

And because my dad could see how passionate I was about writing songs, when I was about 11, he surprised me with the best present I could ask for – a Studio 100 hi-fi system. I had no idea what to do with it, but I knew I wanted it. It looked the business with all the faders and microphones with different coloured foam capsules and it had a record deck on top and two twin cassette decks. It was like every Christmas I'd ever had all rolled into one and, as I dedicated myself to understanding how all these buttons and microphones worked, I grew more confident. I would experiment by using two tapes, recording the lead vocal on one and putting that in the top deck, recording a new harmony over that on the second tape, replacing it with the first tape, then recording over the second one again … and, in this way, I stacked the vocals up and up until it made a song. With my eclectic collection of vinyls and my Studio 100, my world had now opened up entirely, and there was nothing that gave me greater satisfaction and pleasure than spending hours and hours in my room giving myself over to mixing and writing and learning how to DJ.

Southampton was a great source of new music, but I had other ways of getting new sounds. My mum, too, could see *exactly* what all this meant to me and, every six weeks or so, we'd take the train to London Waterloo to two places that sold records that couldn't be found in my hometown. Going up to London was a big enough deal so, when we'd switch to the Northern Line at Waterloo and then change on to the Victoria Line, by the time we came out in Brixton, I could have fallen over with giddy anticipation. We'd head first to Red Records and then on to Solar Records, where the owner would spend loads of quality time with me, playing these unique mixes that you couldn't find *anywhere* else: a cappellas from one song, beats from another, melodies from one more. I was so excited when I bought them because I knew that no one in South-ampton would have them. I'd use my pocket money, but my mum – and every day I am still grateful to her for this – always managed to have an additional few pounds in her pocket to buy those extra ones that she *knew* would make a big difference to me. Even on the train home, I was making up lyrics to lay over the B-side instrumental, the music pulsing through me.

Back in my bedroom, I was still using my Studio 100. I already had a belt-drive record deck which my mum and dad upgraded to a direct-drive Technics SL-1210 for my birthday. This was a big game changer for me. The only thing was that, without a mixer and another deck, I couldn't really use it. However, just knowing I had it was enough of an incentive for me to save up – from doing odd jobs with my dad and not spending any pocket or birthday money, to selling chocolate at school, which I'll tell you about later – and, eventually, I was able to buy a mixer. Then my parents made my dreams come true, surprising me with another deck for Christmas that year.

Through word on the street, I got noticed. One day, a message on my pager pinged – this was back in the day – asking if I wanted to do a session on PCRS 105.3. 'People's Choice Radio Station' was a pirate radio station that played R&B, hip-hop and bashment (Jamaican dancehall music) broadcasting from unknown locations in the tower blocks across my neighbourhood of St Mary's. Man, I was 13 and wanted *nothing* more than to be a part of it.

When that message popped up, and there was no warning other than a couple of hours – 'Albion Towers tonite 7–8' – I lugged my box of records up to whatever block and whatever floor they were on and got down to it. You never really knew who was actually running the show and, when you pitched up, there'd be different people every time, swapping in and out. I couldn't get enough of it. DJs and techies crammed into a tiny room, cables coming in through a window that had been hooked up to an antenna on the roof of the building, all joined into a load of hi-fi and stereo equipment, two Technics 1210s, a mixer, a microphone and boxes and boxes of records everywhere. Heaven.

I don't think they ever knew I was as young as I was. I'd do my set, taking it as seriously as if I were on a legal radio station. It was all legit to me. I wanted to learn. I wanted to be in there and I needed to make every moment of my one-hour slot count. You were in and out, no time for messing around or getting to know anyone. You could cut the edgy vibe, nerves jangling, an undercurrent of anticipation that at any moment there was going to be a knock at the door and the police would be there to shut us down, confiscate everything and haul whoever was in the room down to the station. One day, I got word that there *had* been a raid and everything – all the equipment, everyone's records – had been seized. That scared me; my records were my life, my most precious and prized possessions, and I'd be nowhere without them. When I heard this, I knew I couldn't risk it, so I dipped out of the pirate radio game. My heart was so heavy and I was miserable for days, wondering if I'd made the right decision, even though I knew deep down that I had. Waiting for my pager to flash up, doing my hour sporadically across the year had been the most thrilling experience of my life. I'd seen loads, learned more and I'd wanted to do it forever.

PCRS had given me a taste of live DJing, and I liked it. It boosted my confidence. When my friends and I would jam to Boyz II Men's 'End of the Road' at school, they would ask me to sing all the ad libs and high notes, and I'd get bolder each time, until I was proper performing. I'd always get a good

It felt great to be able to give something of myself and see the way others reacted.

feeling from the way they were responding. It felt great to be able to give something of myself and see the way others reacted. Looking back, because I was expressing what was true to me and had fun while doing it, it was a bonus that others seemed to like it. It felt balanced and their reaction made it extra special, but it wasn't the *reason* I made music.

ONCE IN A LIFETIME

At 14, I entered a songwriting competition for Damage, an all-boys R&B band that my mum and I loved. She'd read in the inside cover of their most recent single that they were going to release a cover of Eric Clapton's 'Wonderful Tonight' and were calling for an original track for the B-side. This was my moment – I fired up my Studio 100, started bouncing vocals back and forth on tape until I got something good, called it 'I'm Ready' and sent it off.

The next thing we knew, it was a bit like that Billy Elliot moment when the letter arrives. Billy's at school, and his brother and dad look at it, unable to bear the thought of not opening it, but knowing that's a boundary they can't cross as it's addressed to Billy. When I got back at teatime, my mum held out an envelope to me and told me to open it. When I read 'Congratulations …' I had to hand it back to her to make sure I was reading it right. I *had*. I'd *won*. And not only were Damage going to record my entry, but, having heard me sing, they had invited me to London to add my backing vocals in with theirs.

When I met Damage I could tell they were genuinely surprised I was so young. I was on top of the world and it made me even happier to see how made up my mum was to meet the band. The single went to number two in the charts and, while I like to think it was because of the B-side, it may just have been because 'Wonderful Tonight' is one of the best songs ever written.

Back home, I'm not going to lie, it was cool walking into a music store and seeing the CD on sale. I got some kudos from my friends and it was a good feeling knowing that my music had reached further than my schoolmates, my mum, my dad and my nan. From then on, I worked even harder mixing my tapes. Right from an early age, I've liked the neatness of organisation, and there was something completely natural for me in gravitating from making and mixing songs to laying them down on cassettes, copying those cassettes, neatly writing out the song order on each one and giving them out to friends and family. And maybe there was something fresh in them, something that appealed about the way I mixed different sounds, because somehow or other they got passed around and I loved that. I loved that all the hard work I was putting into mixing and laying vocals, making the cassette covers and designing the track list inlays, was giving people the vibe.

Because I now had a bit of a reputation, I got into selling my mixtapes locally with help from shops, like Bego's the local barbers, where I went to get my hair cut, soaking up the West Indian vibes – reggae blasting out of their speakers and clients sitting on plastic white chairs inside and out, chatting and chilling. I'd tell them about my latest tape and, because I had the gift of the gab, they'd end up taking one and playing it. Then the next time I'd go in, there'd be more people asking me for one.

My first taste of live performance was at my dad's West Indian Community Club where he was one of the chairmen. I'd go with him to watch him play fiery games of dominoes, the speed and smash of the tiles on the table something that I can still see and hear to this day. But best of all were the nights when the DJs came in and, one summer evening, one of them – DJ Flash – saw me watching, taking in his set. I asked if I could jump on the microphone and, as he played one of my favourite tracks – Horace Brown's 'Things We Do For Love' – I ad-libbed and sung around it, and I could sense the atmosphere around the room lifting. People were listening, dancing and responding to my vibe and, again, I won't lie, it was the best feeling ever; like I was doing what was true to myself, yet pleasing others at the same time.

When you're passionate about something, nothing is too much effort. Maybe you know what I mean. It gives you such a buzz doing what comes naturally, rising up from inside you. Like when I'm swimming – something I had to learn, but with practice got better at and can now do without effort but with intense pleasure. There's also something about our childhood innocence – a little high-five to that untarnished place we come from – in doing something for the sake of it and not because we are self-conscious, doing it to *achieve* something tangible, or coming up against the world of expectation and achievement.

DJ Flash and I got along well and he invited me to be his MC, which meant I was now on the mic, in front of hundreds of people in clubs. I was on a roll and started going by the name of MC Fade – a name I'd chosen for two reasons: my ability to seamlessly fade one track into another and Bego's trademark fade in my hair. There was something in it for both of us as Flash would let me play for ten minutes at the end of his set. Pretty quickly, I worked out a way of getting a bit longer by telling him that a woman in the crowd – and I'd point vaguely in the direction of 'out there' – had been looking at him all evening and, if he wanted to go and chill by the bar and buy her a drink, I'd man the decks. Let's just say it didn't not work.

For the next couple of years, with Flash chaperoning and me carrying his heavy boxes of records, we were regulars at the clubs around the south coast. And the more time I spent in front of the crowd in my own right, the more confident I became. In time, I lost the 'MC' and started to call myself 'DJ', sticking to Fade as 'Flash and Fade' sounded so good together.

As I continued to collect vinyls from all over, my own record boxes started to fill up with priceless gems. Soon, my collection was worth its weight in gold and had become somewhat of a talking point among other DJs as well as Flash. Back in those days, DJs were the go-to people for new sounds. They had the promos way before the track was going to be available commercially, so there'd always be great banter on who found what record and who got which remix first when we'd meet in the local record shops on delivery day. I always loved it when 'DJ T-Bone' from Manchester, who I became friends with after playing many of the same venues, used to drop by my flat when he was in town. We'd talk about what new stuff we were both playing and always ended up having competitions to see who could mix the records back-to-back the fastest. He would also be eager to get his hands on the exclusive records I'd freshly found on my travels.

'Where'd you get that?' he'd ask. 'Nah man, I need that, I've been looking for that one everywhere.'

Without even missing a beat, I'd hit back with: 'OK, I'll swap my Faith Evans for that new Jade record I see you've got over there', akin to those days when you'd have one of those shimmering silver Panini football stickers that you knew were hard to find, but were always ready to swap for the right one. And because some of my records had come from my trips I still made up to Brixton, I'd also add 'and maybe give me a little extra tenner for that on top', which never failed to make me smile when he'd succumb to my savvy bartering skills.

By now, I was at college taking an NVQ in Electronics, which I'd taken up as it was the closest thing to music production on the curriculum – which back then was more about how the metal was forged to make a trumpet than it was how Dr Dre made his productions sound so good. I also figured that learning the electronics would get me closer to circuit boards and closer to working in Richer Sounds around the corner once I'd finished college – they had some wicked equipment there. I'd be near decks, I'd be near speakers and maybe I'd even get a little discount.

During this time, I was busier than ever making my own mixtapes, religiously tuning into *The Lick with Trevor Nelson*, checking out the newest R&B artists he was showcasing and any previously-unheard remixes I could feature on my tapes. It was on his show that I first heard Aaliyah's 'Are You That Somebody', which remains one of my favourite tracks of all time. Every day, instead of going to class, I'd be found in the library. 'Craig, you're really getting in your studying,' my friends would say. But little did they know that I was rinsing out the paper and printer cartridges making the biggest effort getting those tape covers looking great – guillotining, laminating, getting the blurb just right. '*This CD is a compilation of tracks that are blowing up in '98,*' I wrote, '*progressively changing the way in which you, the listener, enjoy the R&B music. Featuring new and soon-to-be-released tracks, DJ Fade is able to keep you right up to date with all your favourite music, so just turn up the volume and enjoy the freshest sounds mixed by one of the south's best.*'

The thing about my mixtapes was that I rarely got to see the effect of them on people as they played them. At Bego's, even if my mixtape was playing, the guys sitting around gossiping weren't really listening, they were just hearing it. It was only when I started to DJ around the clubs that I saw how people truly reacted – mostly through how they got down when dancing to the way I'd sing and ad lib to make the transitions from song to song more unique. That was when I could *see* that I was bringing people some pleasure. I was learning so much being in the clubs and seeing what made people come alive, checking out the vibe.

REWIND

After playing with Flash for a few months, I was given some gigs of my own, including at Old Orientals where there were two floors going at the same time: R&B and hip-hop downstairs; garage and house upstairs. And upstairs is where I first heard the Artful Dodger – a garage duo, then consisting of Mark Hill and Pete Devereux. I liked their sound – 'speed garage' as it was known; a soulful R&B vocal over these skippy beats. And they were playing one song in particular, Scott Garcia's 'It's a London Thing', a classic garage tune from back then, but what they were doing made it feel like I was experiencing something so new, so fresh. Later that night, I introduced myself to Mark and we developed this rapport. He told me about his studio in Ocean Village, which was five minutes from my flat. It turned out that he had loads of music and I had loads of lyrics; he was looking for a vocalist and I was looking for music – and it was just this beautiful synergy where we both looked at each other and he said, 'Do you want to come down to the studio and maybe we could do something?'

That was a pivotal conversation. Looking back, it's true to say that everything took off from that moment. Walking from my flat to Ocean Village a few days later, the fresh air of the sea and the boats bobbing about in the marina, I was feeling the vibe. As soon as I walked into his studio, it felt like I'd come home, but here there was proper equipment, the *real* stuff, in a soundproof room. Mark was so welcoming and he played me a couple of tracks that he and Pete were working on, one of which was 'Something'. It connected with me straight away, so we worked on my vocals, recorded it and, from one moment to the next, I was on that song, on a vinyl – 'Artful Dodger featuring Craig David'. It felt sweet to be on a vinyl – like I'd made it. And then, quite literally, Mark and Pete went up to London to distribute the track in the clubs up there and to the record shops, like the ones I'd been going to in Brixton, and something began to build. I was just happy to be on a track, but when I was getting people around me saying they had come down from London where they'd heard 'Something' on pirate radio stations or been at a club and the DJ had spun it four times back to back, I was blown away. The garage scene was really starting to take off by this time – I loved picking up the latest Garage Nation tape packs whenever they were released. Going into the BIC club in Bournemouth and seeing DJ Spoony, part of the Dreem Teem, who were so instrumental in building that distinctive sound, is something that has stayed with me down the years.

Something was bubbling and, again, I teamed up with the Artful Dodger and recorded 'What Ya Gonna Do', laying my vocals over that syncopated, two-step beat. Before I knew it, I got a call from Public Demand, the label that had invested in the record and done a licencing deal for it, asking me if I wanted to come to London and start doing some live appearances. So there I was – in the Colosseum club in Vauxhall – performing it to a packed house, and then all these pirate radio stations in London were playing it and there was this buzz around us, which we decided to drill down on and capture the vibe to record our next track: 'Rewind'.

'Rewind' nearly didn't make it out into the world. On the day we thought we had it down, we recorded it onto a TDK D90 cassette to play it on the car stereo, something we liked to do to hear how the song would sound outside the studio. It was mostly great, but we wanted to make some tweaks and I wanted to do some extra ad libs, so we went straight back to work. In the studio, I tossed the cassette onto the sofa we sprawled across when we were coming up with ideas for songs and fired the computer back up. As we chatted away watching the boot-up process on the screen, it suddenly went blank and then reappeared in a weird, glitchy fashion. Then, out of nowhere, those dreaded file error messages flashed up, one after the other. Telling each other not to freak out, we freaked out, pressing the return key on the keyboard over and over again, until there were about a million file errors on top of each other. We pressed some more keys, until the error messages had disappeared, expecting to see a full screen of pretty wave forms, but instead there were just a few random hi-hats from the song. And then we realised that this was all that was left of the song we'd been working on for weeks – often late into the night. Despondently, I crashed down onto the sofa and landed on something hard. I lifted up a cushion and there, glowing like a golden ticket, was our TDK D90. I picked up the tape and carried it, with all the reverence I'd have given a Wonka Golden Ticket, over to the tape deck. I placed it in the cradle, gently shut the door, pressed play and waited. Out came a perfectly preserved version of the song. We were saved.

Early the next morning, the sun not yet up, after piecing the song back together to its original form, I walked home listening to the track on my Walkman. I remember the moment when the bass hit just right and I got that feeling I can't articulate. It was like everything was aligned and all was OK with the world. Again, Mark and Pete and MC Alistair, a friend of ours from back home, did their magic up in the London clubs and I went up to do my first performance of the song in Camden Palace. Driving up from Southampton in my mate Clinton's nifty yellow Fiesta, his Jamaican flag displayed in the back and the subwoofer in the boot pumping out, we heard the track on a pirate radio station and, buzzing, joined in at the top of our voices as we rolled up the M3.

By August 1999, 'Rewind' was yet to be officially released, but it was going down a storm with DJs. I was 16 years old and gaining in confidence, London now on my horizon. So I decided to go to the Notting Hill Carnival – my first time going to the iconic cultural event I'd heard so much about. And it was there that I experienced a moment that I'll never forget, a moment in which I could feel that my life was changing in the most unexpected and glorious way.

I travelled up with Alistair and a few of our friends from home and we posted up at a few different sound systems, soaking up the atmosphere. We decided to try to roll behind one of them as we felt we'd be able to take in more that way. Oh man, it was the food for my soul that I'd craved; towering speakers stacked on top of each other, bass so low that you almost lifted up out of your shoes and tweeters so crisp that you could hear every word.

Lost in the moment, I realised that I'd become separated from everyone. With the streets packed and no way of finding them, I decided to make my way back to our starting position, knowing we'd all drift back there sooner or later. So there I was, on this hot summer's day, dancing up a storm alone, taking it all in, vibing up the atmosphere, my mind and body alive to the music; the colourful waves of the procession going by, the smells of Caribbean cooking wafting over me. When I came to this spot where the sound system was the loudest of them all and had by far the heaviest bass I had ever heard, I stopped as I heard this familiar vocal. I thought, 'It can't be …', but then, as I heard '*making moves, yeah, on the dance floor*', I knew it was. They were playing 'Rewind'. It sounded unbelievable and it hadn't even got to the bass drop. And all of a sudden, under that bright blue sky of sunshine, all these beautiful people around me started singing my name and yet no one knew it was me. And then the bass hit. Everyone was so wild with abandonment, so in the moment, that the DJ ended up reloading the track, playing it five times in a row. People were losing their minds to the song; it was like they'd have given their life to keep dancing and singing to it and, what was so amazing for me as I watched, was that no one knew – nor would have believed – that *I* was Craig David. I was a ghost witnessing the purest reaction to my music. As I looked on, I experienced a moment of such happiness, I can only describe it as pure euphoria. I was watching a crowd of people dancing and singing to something I'd helped create and I knew that this moment would stay with me for the rest of my life.

Down the years, with all the good, and not-so-good, things that have happened in between, I realise that that moment was pure. That there was this perfect synchronicity between who I was at my truest self and how that truth had brought pleasure to others. That since being a boy, by having held space for my music and my creative side, I'd not only made myself happy, but had managed to bring others along with me.

I knew that this moment would stay with me for the rest of my life.

CHAPTER THREE
Heartline

From about the age of eight, my weight grew faster than my height. I'd always enjoyed my food and, in particular, I loved the care and affection with which my nan nourished me. Through my years at primary school, she'd always be there to pick me up at the end of the day.

You might remember how ridiculously hungry you were after school. To be fair, it is a long time from lunch to the end of the school day and, if you were anything like me, you'd have been tearing around the playground during afternoon break, so be ravenous by the time that last bell rang. Grabbing my coat from my hook in the sweaty cloakroom, I'd race out to the school gates and there my nan would be, smiling and waving, and in her bag I knew were the most delicious sandwiches ever known. Whatever was in them – cheese, jam, ham – they tasted like no other sandwich anyone else has ever made me. I used to think the magic ingredient was her special sprinkle, a secret known only to her.

Once at her house, I would head straight for the fridge for a chocolate dessert – a mousse that, again, I thought was unique to my nan, and then, around about teatime, the pièce de résistance: her special chicken stew. Now, I still don't know to this day how she made this stew – the meat was lean and the sauce … that thick, delicious sauce that I still taste in my memory to this day. My mum tried to make it a few times, but it just didn't hit. My nan was like an alchemist – the only one who could work the stew magic.

Unsurprisingly, I was not as lean as the meat I was eating. But in that way of blissful childhood innocence, I wasn't really conscious of being a bit chubbier than the other kids around me until a PE lesson in the school hall one afternoon towards the end of the final term of Year 3. We'd get changed at the edge of the hall and, aged eight, you had to concentrate on getting your uniform into a little pile, getting your PE kit out and changing into your Woolworths' plimsolls. In doing my best to be quick and efficient, I hadn't noticed someone taking my PE shorts. I had on my little Aertex shirt, which thankfully came down over my pants, and was frantically searching for my shorts, when I heard some laughs coming from the other side of the hall.

It soon became clear that someone had thrown my shorts behind the wooden wall bars of the gym apparatus. I pulled my shirt down as far as it would go – calculating that I didn't need to put my school trousers back on as I'd get into trouble for being slow – and ran over to retrieve my shorts. Touching the wall bars in any way was strictly forbidden without the teacher giving permission, but she was busy instructing a group of girls to get a bunch of equipment out, so I stretched through the bars to get my shorts. However, I couldn't reach them so I decided the only option was to push myself through the narrow gap between the rungs. Total self-destruct. I found myself so deeply wedged in between the bars that I couldn't get myself out. I was too chubby to get through to where my shorts were and, by this time, my classmates had clocked on, the boys jeering at me for being stuck, the girls pointing at my bare legs. With all the noise, the teacher marched over. Realising that I wasn't going to get out, she tactfully, but so painfully for me, released the bars from the wall so I could escape. To spare me any further distress, she reached around and picked up my shorts and told me to go and get them on over on the other side of the hall. Her kindness made my eyes prick, but I jammed my fingers into the palms of my hands and willed myself not to cry.

I felt shame like *never* before. The humiliation of that moment has stayed with me through the years. It was the first time that I'd ever been self-conscious of my body and I can still feel the visceral sense of embarrassment that flooded my whole being. I put on my shorts and had no choice but to join in the warm-up star jumps, but inside I was burning, crushed and disgusted with myself. Of course, by the end of the lesson the focus was on someone else who had managed to get into trouble or become the target of some other prank and, while I somehow got to the end of primary school with my outer self intact, the wound of this incident cut deep. We all need to be seen, but to be seen for the wrong reasons can damage us more profoundly than we realise at the time.

I always got on well with the girls in my class and, as we got older and boys and girls became more self-conscious around each other, I became that guy who the girls came to for advice, but never the one they liked in the way that it mattered back then. I was the one they still talked to, the one they told who they had their sights set on, who they wanted me to get a message to. And then, when things didn't work out, I was the

We all need to be seen, but to be seen for the wrong reasons can damage us more profoundly than we realise at the time.

one whose shoulder they cried on. But I was never the one to get the message and that went deep too.

By the time I got to secondary school, I became more self-conscious that my trousers never quite fitted right and I was used to puffing out my shirt so it didn't hug my body. I was at an all-boys comprehensive now and had no trouble making friends or even playing football well enough to get into the school team. I seemed to have learned to move well despite my heaviness.

I was popular too for one special chocolate-related reason. When I'd started school, I'd realised that, by the time we had our mid-morning break and had access to the vending machines, we were hungry and we weren't prepared to wait in queues to get our sugar rush. So, every Saturday, I'd go down to the market and buy up a whole load of chocolate with sell-by dates that were fast approaching and would sell them to my year group first thing each morning. This combined two of my passions – making some extra money to buy vinyls and equipment and my love for *Charlie and the Chocolate Factory*, a movie that I'd comfort-watched again and again for years with my mum. As a kid, I'd alternated between wanting to be Charlie or Willy Wonka, and so selling chocolate at a reduced rate like this spoke to my childhood dreams.

Because I had such a sweet tooth and didn't always sell all of my weekly stock, I became a bit too fond of Boosts and king-size Mars bars, but, as I moved up the school and we hung around with the girls from our sister school, I noticed that they went for the slimmer guys. This, combined with the fact that I was beginning to get out there in the clubs as DJ Fade, made me more self-conscious and, one morning before break, as I held a soon-to-be-out-of-date Crunchie up to my open mouth, I had this sort of epiphany – that I didn't need to eat what I didn't sell and that I should try to shift my excess weight.

I was playing a lot of badminton in those days at the local sports centre. My dad enjoyed it too and sometimes we'd double up and play against a couple of my friends. The sports centre also had a gym, so I started to use it, running on the treadmills. My nan had stopped picking me up and so I wasn't going back to hers for sandwiches, stews, desserts (and more) every day. I've always been disciplined when I put my mind to it and, once I decide on a course of action, I tend to stick with it. So, with less food, throwing in an extra bar to my loyal customers, and more exercise, I got lighter and, between that and my music, the girls started noticing me. And I was there to be seen, ripe and ready for my first kiss. I didn't have to wait long.

KEY TO MY HEART

All through middle school I'd had a crush on a girl called Shelley and did everything I could for her to notice me. She was the kind of girl, with her dazzling smile, who had me doing a dozen bicycle kicks in our lunchtime football matches, mashing up my whole uniform, just hoping, on the off chance, that she'd see one of them and be impressed by my skills. Somehow, my persistence seemed to pay off as, one day, she agreed to come swimming with me on a double date with my friend Michael and his girlfriend Rachel.

After a splash around in the pool, some Quavers and a hot chocolate, we all started walking back home along the long, grey path that joined the swimming baths to the high street. Michael and Rachel peeled off for a kiss and, as Shelley and I found ourselves alone, she smiled at me and I could feel my heartbeat starting to quicken. She stepped closer, closer than she'd ever stepped before, as if she was inviting me into her sacred space. As she leaned in, I leaned in and, before our lips met, the air stood still and I thought, *wow*, this *is the moment when my dreams of kissing the girl I've been dreaming of kissing for so long are going to come true.*

It was every part of the perfect I'd imagined – the softness of her lips, the smell of her perfume, her hair still dripping wet through my fingers; it was magical. What must have been only minutes seemed like a lifetime. And that walk home after saying our sweet goodbyes felt like nothing I had ever experienced before. The same path I had walked a hundred times before was now like something out of *The Wizard of Oz*: vibrant, full of life and beautiful.

What had changed? Why was everything now so vivid? Why did I feel so different? The answer was love. Life had taken on a different beauty and, even though things didn't quite work out as I'd hoped for me and Shelley, I lived for weeks with the sacredness of that kiss. The thrill of it, the pleasure, the acceptance of me as someone desirable was all new. That kiss came from my soul. Nearly thirty years later, it's still somewhere inside my heart, a part of me always.

As significant as that kiss was, nothing prepared me for Nicky and the arrow of love that shot through my heart when I was 17 and finishing my NVQ in Electronics. I'd gone from this all-boys environment to a mixed college after GCSEs and Nicky was the girl everybody was talking about. She came from 'outside town' from a *house* in the suburbs and was *driven* into the city centre on weekends, where she hung out with us. She was stunning, with luminous skin and clear, bright eyes. Her hair was mesmerising – curly one Saturday, straight the next – and she had the most beautiful lips I'd ever seen.

Around her, I felt expansive. I felt open. I felt both alert, as if the world was in sharper focus, and dreamy-drunk, like I was stumbling around in this haze of love, my inhibitions banished. It was a beautiful, beautiful feeling and I loved the vibes that came off me when I was around her. I was intoxicated and there was nothing I wouldn't have done for her.

But there were other guys around, even talk of an ex-boyfriend who could show up at any time, so I had to step up fast. By this time, I was already DJing, had been on the Damage CD and was starting to be noticed a bit more around town, so

Clinton and I decided to put on an under-18s club night that we called 'What You Want (What You Need)'. I thought: if I can get Nicky to come, that's my chance. It will be what she wants and I'll be what she needs. Clinton and I went full out with the publicity, printing posters, laminating the tickets, putting out flyers, and we'd sold half the capacity when I found out that the biggest club in Southampton was having an under-18s night at the same time. That was gutting, as I was sure that Nicky and her sophisticated best friend would choose that one over ours.

As it got closer to the event, we managed to sell most of our tickets, but I still didn't know whether Nicky was going to show up. Come the night, I dressed to impress anyway. I was big into Usher at the time and his thing was these ski goggles that he wore on top of his beanie, a white puffer jacket and matching trousers and this big chain around his neck. That, I decided, was how Nicky would want to see me.

We'd rigged up this sort of stage, the place was lively and the DJ was playing some warm-up music. As I got ready, Clinton hissed at me, 'Craig, Craig. Nicky's here, she's *here.*' Out I went, embracing my full Usher, microphone in hand, 'Nice & Slow' at the ready: '*It's seven o'clock on the dot …*' I had this rose – a real red rose, nothing fake or plastic – in my hand and I walked to the front of the stage, my R&B vibe smooth, and there, right in my sightline and by some miracle, was Nicky. I looked at her and she looked at me, and it was literally as though everyone else in that room disappeared.

'Nicky,' I ad-libbed, handing her the rose, 'I see you there, let me dedicate this one to you.' And I eased back into the song, nice and slow, with more passion than I'd ever sung before, and I could see she felt it. This tremendous vibration buzzed between us and, when I'd finished singing, the crowd went wild. Our love vibe had sweetened the whole place.

After the gig, I didn't get the chance to speak to her for long, but it was long enough for her to say, 'Wow, that was amazing' and for me to ask her out. She said, 'Yeah, I'll call you tomorrow' and I was buzzing and burning. Sure, I was sweating big time in my beanie hat, goggles and nylon puffer gear, but I was hot with love and anticipation for what was to come.

You know that Police song, 'Walking on the Moon'? That was me. All through the next week, I felt giddy and dizzy, astonished that Nicky had seen me and liked what she'd seen. For a while it felt like my insecurities of being the one who no one fancied flew away. I was no longer that chubby little kid, in his own little world of hi-fis. I had been *seen*.

So, the next Saturday, after she was dropped off in town, we went to McDonald's, our mouths on fire from the molten apple pie lava and the promise of a kiss after. 'Nice and slow' was still our vibe. When we were with our friends, her hand was next to mine, our arms brushed up against each other's. In the week we spoke on the phone a bit, but these were pre-mobile days and I was apprehensive about her parents picking up and quizzing me on who I was.

I was no longer that chubby little kid, in his own little world of hi-fis.

Instead, I spent a week making a mixtape – *DJ Fade's Bump & Grind Collection Vol 2*; '*for all those addicted to love*', assuring my listener that '*this is sure to satisfy your every need. Yes, be prepared for things to get hot. Hot like fire.*' The next Saturday, hot off my deck, I gave Nicky the first copy.

The high street was one thing, McDonald's – where I'd had a part-time Saturday job since starting college – was another. But I had bigger plans than using the many Happy Meal vouchers I'd rescued from the trash behind the kitchens. As a treat, my mum and I sometimes ate at Nick's, a proper Greek restaurant. The food was tasty and it was a definite step up from a Big Mac. For days, I imagined Nicky and I sitting opposite each other for a whole evening, talking and getting close. Finally, I summoned up the courage to ask her, risking the landline. 'No,' she said before I'd even got to the name of the restaurant. 'I can't make it and I'm not free for a while after, either. Maybe we'll see each other around sometime.'

Oh man. No need to second-guess my intuition after I heard that tone in her voice. This was telling me that the vibe was off, the 'nice' was no longer so nice and the 'slow' was grinding to a halt. I could feel the despair rising in my chest and called Clinton. He intuited that this was a love emergency – 'Wow, that's unreal,' he said, 'she's hot for you, we can sort it out.' He knew where Nicky lived so he drove me straight over. He parked outside her house and told me he'd wait. It was a warm evening and, as I approached her front door, I could hear music drifting out of her bedroom window. And then I heard my voice – DJ Fade fading across one song into the next – and I thought, wow, that's my mixtape. She's playing my mixtape so she must be thinking about me.

I rang the doorbell, feeling good – about myself and about the situation. Maybe I misread her meaning when she told me she'd see me around. Though this sounded like some vague and distant time, maybe she meant like usual, like this Saturday. As I was standing there, my life-with-Nicky flashing through my heart, I saw this figure coming down the stairs. The front door was made of frosted glass, but I could make out that this was a guy wearing only boxer shorts. Without seeing his face, I knew *exactly* who he was. Somewhere that ex-boyfriend of hers had always been lurking in the back of my mind.

'What d'you want?' he shouted, not opening the door.

I pressed my face closer – 'I just want to speak to Nicky,' I said, and I could hear how lame I sounded.

'She doesn't wanna speak to you,' he said, but then I could make out Nicky behind him – and, even in my panic, I felt relieved that she was dressed.

'Nick,' I shouted. 'Can I speak to you? Just a few minutes. I can see what's going on. It's cool. But can I just talk to you?'

My heart was pounding and I heard him say, 'Nicky, go back upstairs' and she took that opportunity to disappear. In the silence, I could still hear my tape playing, the mix and the fade into the mix, and it sounded good. Maybe he heard that too, as he disappeared and then reappeared and, like in some bad horror movie, I could make out the silhouette of a knife. A sudden feeling of shame began to cloud my judgement and, for one moment, I actually started to puff up my chest to try to redeem some ounce of my dented pride, but, as I did, all I could hear over the pounding of my heart was a voice in my head saying, *Craig you're a lover not a fighter, get out of here, what the hell are you doing?*, so I turned and ran for it, hoping Clinton was ready to bail. When we got back to my flat, we called a friend to check on Nicky and see that she was OK – she was, we later heard – and, with that, my first experience of love was over and my first experience of heartbreak had begun.

That night, when I shut my eyes, I had calm, sweet, heavenly dreams about Nicky, dreams in which it was all OK. It was like I was floating on a cloud and, even in this semi-conscious state, I knew I didn't want to wake up. So, when I did and the harsh light of the next day hit me, I was gutted. As my eyes opened, my beautiful dream quickly vanished behind the invisible veil and only the bleak reality of the situation was left. I swear I felt at that moment my heart break. It was like I could feel it crack and then, just as swiftly, I guess so it didn't shatter into pieces, it closed, shutting itself away.

I had no idea how to express what I was feeling and I'd never felt a pain in my heart like this before. I was crying uncontrollably and all I could think was what had I done to cause this, what had I done for this to go so wrong? Not knowing what to do to shake this feeling or how to take the edge off, I just reached for all I ever knew that seemed to relax me – my microphone and song book – and poured my heart out and recorded a song. At first, even this felt useless, but it seemed like the more I sang, the more I began to relax. I used the instrumental of an R&B quartet called L.S.G. (Levert, Sweat and Gill) which had been on the mixtape that Nicky had been listening to and put my words over it. It was the only way I could process what was going on. The melody melancholic, the chorus simple and to the point: '*I couldn't sleep last night, it didn't feel right, what you done to me Baby ...*'

MY LOVE DON'T STOP

We've all had our hearts broken in one form or another. And time really is a healer – or maybe a great anaesthetic. It was my first taste, too, that heartbreak is not *all* bad. It inspired me to write more music and it gave my lyrics some of the messed-up spice of life. Up till then, I'd been inspired by the chivalrous tone of the R&B I loved – a sort of throw-down-your-coat-so-your-girl-can-walk-over-the-puddle vibe – and a kind of idealised romantic vision of love that came from going to an all-boys school. Girls were a bit 'other-worldly', spotted on the bus on the way home or in the high street on Saturdays, but pretty much out of our league. I did need to learn what real life and relationships with real people were actually like – that love is messy.

I can say now, looking back on over two decades of relationships since that first memory of love, that I have continued to throw myself into my music, to put all my love into my music, to explore love through music rather than open my heart to love in real life.

If you listen to 'One More Time' from my album *Following My Intuition*, you might not be surprised to know that, while it sounds like the song is about my relationship with a woman – '*can't be without your love*' – it's also a love song about my relationship with music.

Though I've honoured that time and the love I had for my music during my heartbroken-teen years, I don't think I realised how closed off to love I was and how music seemed to be my only safe place to fully open my heart.

Music has always been there for me; it is the love that has always had my back. Music is constant and giving. Maybe you have it with the stuff in life that you feel passionate about – being in full flow on the football pitch or the rhythm of writing or painting. For me, nothing hits quite like the feeling when the melody connects with the lyrics, when the song comes together and there's this euphoria and I'm right in it, intoxicated and happy. That was definitely how I felt writing my first album *Born To Do It*, in 2000, when I was 19. The whole experience of writing and recording was like being hit by love, euphoria, the excitement of a new relationship all the way through. So I can see now, for me, it was easy to ignore that my life was missing meaningful love from a relationship.

Music has always
been there for me;
it is the love that has
always had my back.

CHAPTER FOUR
Born to Do It

After 'Rewind' was released in November 1999 and shot into the charts at number two, life became even more surreal. Mark Hill and I were at Ocean Village one morning, laying down some tracks, when Paul Widger, a music manager from London, arrived with a young singer-songwriter who he wanted to try out with the Artful Dodger. One thing led to another and we played him two songs we'd been working on, one of which was 'Walking Away'. As he was listening, I could see his eyes light up like a Christmas tree. He told us, 'Let me take this and play it to a few people', so we burned him a CD with a couple of other tracks and off he went back up to London.

The next thing I knew there was a whole lot of attention on me. It turned out that there were a 'few people' who 'seemed quite interested', so Paul sent me a train ticket and I bought a new Topman suit, polished up – and squeezed my feet into – my old school shoes and headed up to London. By this time I had written 'Fill Me In' and, over the next few weeks, I had meetings with several of these 'quite interested' record labels. Unbelievably for me, in the mix of those people interested in signing me was the one-and-only Trevor Nelson, who was now also an A&R for a label called Cooltempo. He had the job of finding new talent and helping nurture their specific sound into a finished project. Unfortunately, things didn't align at the time, but I am forever grateful to him for championing me and my music throughout my career and, to this day, he continues to set the tone of R&B in the UK. One day, as I was coming out of a meeting at Columbia Records, where everything was marble and expensive, and where there were six-foot posters of Mariah Carey on the walls, I had to pinch myself to believe that any of this was happening to me.

These meetings seemed to be on an endless cycle – nothing, it turned out, was as straightforward as signing me on the spot – and so instead of going backwards and forwards from Southampton, it was decided that I should stay at Paul's place in Surrey. I was happy with this. Paul was easy to get on with and we'd spend evenings going over the day's events at his local Indian, where the Peshawari naan was to die for, or at a slightly further away Italian, where I developed my now-infamous love of cheesecake. Other evenings, I'd just chill, working on vocals in the living room while he spent time in his home office or with his family and friends. The atmosphere in the house was happy and loving, and he made me welcome. I missed my bedroom back in Southampton, which had always been a place of containment and security for me, but I spoke to my mum on the phone regularly and I knew it wouldn't be too long before I was home.

Paul was playful and loved pulling pranks, so when, as I sat there finishing off another song, he burst in to tell me that Puff Daddy was on the phone, I played along and said, 'Yeah right, I'll talk to him right now.' He handed me the phone.

'Yo,' came a voice that actually sounded remarkably like Puffy.

'Puffy,' I said, waiting for the prankster to reveal himself now he'd got me.

'Yo, Craig,' he said and launched into praising my work, talking about how much he loved 'Walking Away', while insisting that I be part of the Bad Boy family on his hugely successful Bad Boy Records label. He also dropped in the mix that the private jet was on the tarmac ready to come and pick me up, and all I had to do was say the word. All the while, I played along with the very impressive prank and even gave Paul a wink to say, 'Well done; you nearly got me'. But it was only when the prankster said, 'Can I take that as a yes?', referring to him asking me moments earlier if we had a spoken agreement in place, that the penny dropped. *It can't be*, I thought, but the voice was identical to the one I'd heard on so many Notorious B.I.G. tracks when Puffy would come in with that oh-so-recognisable '... take that, take that, Bad Boy!' intro vocal. Wait up, I thought. This actually *is* Puffy.

It took a few moments for this to sink in. A few weeks before, I'd been an unknown teenager in Southampton, working part-time at McDonald's, finishing my NVQ, having spent years working alone in my bedroom mixing tapes, and now here I was in a music manager's house, having come from meeting with some of the most prestigious record companies in the world, talking to one of my childhood idols, who had called *me* up from New York. It felt sweet and, like that moment at Notting Hill, epic.

In the end, after rounds of meetings in which representatives from several record labels listened to my new songs including 'Walking Away', 'Rendezvous' and a cover of The Human League's 'Human', which had somehow made it onto my demo CD, and my potential and future career was picked over and discussed, sometimes as if I wasn't even in the room, the offers of 'development deals' came in. Loosely translated, this means a singles deal and then development. I couldn't get my head around what that really meant, what they were developing. I'd developed my music, 'Rewind' was a hit and I wanted to move forward with releasing singles and an album.

It was a no-brainer when Colin Lester at Wildstar Records came forward with a record deal. On the basis of the success of 'Rewind' and my demo of 'Walking Away', he was prepared to go the whole way and, because Capital Radio and Telstar

Records were part-owners of Wildstar, this meant a direct route to compilations and radio. Paul was happy with the whole package and I liked Colin's vibe – he was open and communicative, and he made me feel as if *I* owned – and could keep hold of – myself and my talent.

When we signed the deal, it was for an amount that I had never even contemplated as being within my reach. But it wasn't like it was paid into my current account and that was it. Everything suddenly became very formal – accountants, lawyers, signing this, signing that – and it was sometimes hard for me to keep up with it all. I had to rely on others to steer me; as savvy and worldly as I thought I was at 19, of course, in reality, I was wide-eyed and naïve.

WHAT MORE COULD I ASK FOR?

Life was moving fast. In April 2000, I released 'Fill Me In'. When the midweeks – chart positions – came in, Colin called me into his office.

'Do you want the good news or the bad news first?' he asked.

'The bad news, obviously,' I said.

'Craig,' he said, completely deadpan, 'your life is never going to be the same again; everything's changed.'

'That's the bad news?' I said. 'What's the good news then?'

He looked at me and his expression changed. 'Well, the good news is that you're 250,000 copies above number two in the charts. And that number two is held by Destiny's Child. You have a guaranteed Number One.'

Destiny's Child? Beyoncé, whose posters I had ripped out of magazines and Blu-Tacked to my bedroom wall? As cool as I was trying to be, I couldn't hold back. My smile was Garfield level. Colin handed me the phone. 'Do you want to call your mum?' he asked, and we could have heard her excitement if we'd been on the moon.

And then it was a whirlwind. I was performing on *Top of the Pops* – even the memory of that sends chills down my spine – and I was in hot demand: a lot of features in newspapers and magazines, interviews and performances on radio and TV, acoustics on shows like *Later with Jools Holland* and *TFI Friday* – all that was bringing me to a whole new audience. I went from being a 'rising garage star' to being seen as a song-writer with lyrics and melodies that appealed more widely. Paul had introduced me to Fraser T Smith, a guitarist from near where he lived, who had come to his attention by posting CDs through his letterbox, weekly beats with beautiful guitar melodies over them that he created at a nearby studio. (Fraser and I hit it off big time – we'd end up on the road together for years to come.)

It was at this time that I started gearing up for the release of my second single '7 Days', a song that was to introduce the more R&B side of me to the world. As I prepared for its release, I could feel the excitement from everybody in the team. We had TV performances lined up, radio interview requests coming in and magazine cover shoots booked. From the word go it was all hands on deck and, let me tell you, the deck was full. When it came to the video, my main goal was to find someone who could not only bring the storyline to life, but do it in a fresh, playful way rather than anything too clichéd and obvious. After seeing various treatments, I chose Max & Dania, a director duo who knew my vibe from shooting my 'Fill Me In' video. I'd always loved the movie *Groundhog Day* so when they suggested using a similar vibe where I would experience the same day repeating over and over again, with me waking up at the same time of 11am, with the same weather report on the radio, the same news on TV, then head out for the day to find myself seeing the same people as the day before, I was excited. There was a swerve, though, as, with every new restart of the day, I'd soon start to recognise the familiarity of the events unfolding until I realised that the multitude of obstacles that kept getting in the way of me asking out a girl I meet in a subway could be avoided. To me, using the vibe of this classic movie was genius as it definitely wasn't obvious and was so far from being a clichéd play on just days on end of love-making.

The challenge was to try to pull it all off in under five minutes in a music video. So we jumped into it and started to create all the various scenarios I would face, while making sure that every change we'd make to the repeating day was obvious enough that it would land in the final cut. After shooting the video, it was everything and more than I could have imagined with all the moments of jeopardy packed in there: almost missing the girl at the subway because of my shell toes getting mashed; meeting the girl, but not having my watch when she asks me for the time; having my watch and saving her number into my old-school Nokia, but then finding the petrol gauge in my car on empty … until, finally, everything aligns and we go for a drink. The smile, the confident spring in my step was like something out of Robin Williams' *The Fisher King*, having received the holy grail of numbers and finally cracking the *Groundhog Day* code.

I felt that everyone who saw that memorable scene at the end of the video when I spill my glass of red wine all over my dinner date would somehow relate to a situation that they may have experienced in their own lives and wish that they, too, could have paused the frame, stepped out of the drama, 'rewinded' it (pun intended), then made a few adjustments before stepping back in and pressing play. It's funny as, even at this early stage in my life, I recognised that this moment was not only something cool and cutting-edge for the video, but there was some beautiful wisdom in it. This early 'aha' moment would prove priceless later on in my life and would become a tool that I'd use to step out of the metaphorical movie scene and re-jig how I related with the rest of the cast members, before stepping back in and pressing play again on the movie called life.

With a finished '7 Days' video in the can, it was time to put together the remix package so all the DJs would be set to give their maximum support way upfront, just like those promos I'd buy up in Brixton with my mum. So I jumped in with Full Crew, a UK remix team who I'd loved since we'd worked on 'Part 2' of 'Fill Me In'. I then got in with the legendary garage producer, Sunship, who was the mastermind behind Sweet Female Attitude's 'Flowers', which still to date for me is one of biggest garage records ever. He smashed the remix and knowing that I had the DJs covered felt good given how important they were in supporting artists.

Having got the UK remix package sounding great, I started work on the US ones. Someone I'd always wanted to work with was DJ Premier, the man responsible for countless hits with his group Gang Starr with his partner Guru, who I'd had the pleasure of working with on a song called 'No More' on his *Jazzmatazz* album early in the year. DJ Premier had produced some of my favourite hip-hop records ever – from Nas' 'Nas is Like' and Notorious B.I.G.'s 'Ten Crack Commandments' to Royce Da 5'9"'s 'Boom', to name a few. So you can imagine how gassed I was when I heard that he wanted to remix '7 Days' too and feature Mos Def on it. I had to channel my inner Nate Dogg on the intro 'Oh no' vocal as I knew the vibe would be right, especially as Mos Def's hit of the same name was blowing up in the clubs. Just as I had wrapped up the remix after a short trip to New York to record it over at DJ Premier's studio, I got the call that Irv Gotti also wanted to remix the song.

Talk about being in an R&B/hip-hop dream. Irv Gotti was the producer behind most of Ja Rule and Ashanti's huge songs and he had an idea for a remix for '7 Days'. He sent over an instrumental that he thought would fit and I was super hyped to hear what he had cooked up. When I listened to the instrumental he had sent I was loving what I heard, but at the same time I found it hard to come up with anything new as a topline over it as it was the identical instrumental to one of my favourite Notorious B.I.G. songs ever – 'One More Chance' (remix) featuring Faith Evans, a song that I'd played in my DJ Fade sets. Like any song that goes into the classics pile, as a songwriter I found it especially difficult to find a way to write anything else but the existing melody, so making this instrumental work was always going to be a bit of a non-starter. So I politely said that the instrumental was amazing, but the B.I.G. version was too close for me to be able to write anything new over it and asked if Irv was cool to send some other ideas over. As the release date came closer and there was no new music coming back from Irv, it seemed as if the moment had passed. I always wondered if I had made the right decision in not trying to make the Notorious B.I.G. instrumental work, but it was only when I heard Ashanti's 'Foolish' a few years later, that I weirdly realised it was. Her song used the exact same instrumental that Irv had sent to me for '7 Days' and guess who produced Ashanti's song – you got it in one, Irv Gotti. I realised I may have been a little too hasty to turn that one down seeing how huge Ashanti's version was, yet, on the other hand, I was really happy I did as Ashanti may never otherwise have recorded 'Foolish' and that would have been a shame as I love that song and I'm sure so many of you do too.

In August 2000, I recorded my first album, *Born To Do It*. The title came easily to me. I'd always loved the moment in the movie *Charlie and the Chocolate Factory* right near the beginning when a bunch of children find out that Willy Wonka has invented yet another new chocolate bar, Scrumdiddly-umptious. One of the children is wide-eyed with amazement and asks the sweet shop owner, 'How does he do it?'

'My dear boy,' says the sweet shop owner, 'do you ask a fish how it swims?'

'No,' the boy replies.

'Or a bird how it flies?' the shop owner continues. 'No sirree, you don't. They do it because they were born to do it.'

Maybe I was born to make songs because that album debuted at Number One and ended up selling over 8 million copies worldwide. For a while it held the record for the fastest selling debut album by a British solo act and it got me noticed and nominated. I was being styled, I was being

I was being styled, I was being invited and I was being *seen*.

invited and I was being *seen*. Nigel Melville, my stylist at the time, knew exactly the right EVISU jeans and Adidas shell toes that would complement each other and, now that I was living a little too far away to go for my regular weekly trims at Bego's, I had Five join my team, who not only appeared as my on-screen barber in the '7 Days' video, but was busy getting creative with my actual hair on the road, having me in and out of my beanie cap in what became my signature style of small china bump twists with a crisp fade. The new style was even making it on posters in hairdressers' windows from Ladbroke Grove to Lagos, with young kids asking their hairdresser for a 'Craig David special'.

It was in February 2001 when I found out that I had been nominated for a whopping six BRITs, which included 'Best Male Solo Act', 'Best Single' and 'Best Breakthrough Act'. Not only was I buzzing about this, like Charlie when he found the golden ticket, but I had also been asked to perform at the iconic event. As the days drew closer, a rainbow of euphoria washed over me as I pinched myself thinking *how is this all happening to me? Did I really create all this?*

But this dreamlike disbelief was to be short-lived when I got a call from Colin.

'Hey Craig,' he said. 'Have you seen the papers?'

'No, what's up?' I replied.

'Wait for it,' he said and then read out the headlines splashed across the tabloids: 'Craig David snubbed.' '6 BRITS No Win for CD.'

He explained that the press had got an early leak of the results and the news was legit. At first I was disappointed knowing that there were no shiny BRIT awards at the end of the rainbow, but, as I knew only too well, performing on the night was the pot of gold, a dream for any artist.

That evening, as I sat with my family at the table with representatives from my record company when the award ceremony got underway, I was aware of cameras pointed towards me, ready to catch my reaction as the winners were announced. I had to somehow find an *'I'm cool with it'* vibe each time I didn't win, while simultaneously not smiling too much so that I looked overly happy at losing whenever some-one else's name was announced.

But what happened next was something that I could never have imagined – a run of golden moments that instantly had me break out of any acting and instead captured my heart. As each of the special guests stepped on stage to present awards, and it became clear I was not winning category after category, they all started to show how they felt about it. Dane Bowers of Another Level was the first to show his love as he presented an award wearing a 'Craig woz robbed' T-shirt. Next was Sir Elton John – yes, Sir Elton John – who stepped up on stage and announced, 'If there's a better singer in England than Craig David, then I'm Margaret Thatcher.' Then, to top it all off, U2 took to the stage to perform their hit song 'One' and, when they transitioned spontaneously into my song 'Walking Away', I felt I *had* won all of the six awards; I couldn't believe it. Only a few years before I had written that song in my little flat in Southampton, looking out of my bedroom window for that 'better day', and here I was experiencing one of the best days of my life – looking out from my table at a raft of superstars singing my praises. When the audience responded with cheers to each mention of my name, I felt as though everyone in the building wanted to make it known that I was seen and that my music was being celebrated. And if all this wasn't enough, with a spring in my step I then jumped on stage to perform 'Fill Me In' to rapturous applause, finishing it with a little freestyle rap to mark the occasion. It was in this moment that I learned that, even though I may not technically have won anything, the way my music was making people 'feel', even at this early stage in my career, was something even more profound and beautiful than being given a shiny award.

Later, the awards did come in and they came in thick and fast: 'Best R&B' at the MTV Europe Music Awards, 'Songwriter of the Year' at the Ivor Novello Awards (the UK equivalent of the GRAMMYs) and then there was the Music of Black Origin (MOBO) awards that Kanya King had created to allow for more representation in the music scene by celebrating the breadth of Black Music rather than allowing it all to be pigeonholed as 'Urban'. It was on this stage that I picked up my first ever award – actually three. It felt good to be wearing my red 'Buy British' roll-neck jumper for the occasion as the UK garage and R&B scene was thriving and I wanted the world to know how proud I was to be a part of it.

I was living it all, riding the crest of the wave, up on the top, because it was all new and it was all exciting. There was one evening when I had finished doing an interview with Capital Radio and had to get to my next appearance across Leicester Square to a club called Sound, a 30-second walk away. But there were so many people waiting to see me outside the radio station, shouting for my attention, that I had to be picked up and carried across the road on the shoulders of one of the security guys.

And it wasn't just in the UK that I had gained some fame. I was going abroad to do interviews, mostly on radio stations. I was in France nearly every other week for a while and, in between, I was in Norway, Sweden and Germany. In Paris, on Skyrock, Usher was in the studio at the same time as me.

Usher. My hero. In his beanie. With his chain. Usher, who I'd embodied while trying to impress Nicky at my under-18s club night. But what was unbelievable was that the crowd outside the station were calling out for *me* and I was standing there waving back, thinking, '... but this is Usher'. In the studio, the DJ had caught my fanboy vibe, so he invited us to do a duet together, to freestyle over an instrumental.

'I'm down,' I said, looking at Usher, my heart hammering.

'Yeah,' he said, 'yeah let's vibe', and off I went into a bit of 'You Make Me Wanna', a bit of 'Nice & Slow', and he was harmonising and doing his thing, and I thought if my 14-year-old self could have seen me now, he would have blinked and rubbed his eyes and thought he was seeing some sort of mirage.

In America, I went to the famous House of Blues to do three nights of performances. On the first night, Missy Elliott and Jennifer Lopez came to see the show and I thought, this is *wild*. The second night, Beyoncé came and I thought, this is *ridiculous*. Yet, on the last night, something was about to go down that I could only liken to something you'd expect to happen having rubbed Aladdin's magical lamp. As I performed for my last night in LA, I could see a lot of attention on one particular gentleman in the audience, so I asked for the house lights to go up so I could join in. I looked into the crowd while singing 'Walking Away' and there, singing along, was Stevie Wonder. *Wow, Stevie Wonder*, I thought as I tried to keep my composure and hold the melody of the last chorus. This made me so emotional as I remembered my mum's record collection and her absolute love for Stevie Wonder and his music. I got to meet him at the end of the night when he came into my dressing room with a friend; a friend who was about to put the icing on the incredible three-night-run cake. The friend he'd come with was the legendary music producer Quincy Jones and, if that wasn't enough – to have two legends in front of me praising my performance – it was what Quincy said next that absolutely floored me.

'You know, Craig,' he said, 'MJ's got your album. He loves *Born To Do It*. He's been listening and has given it to all his friends.'

As I smiled and said thank you, it suddenly dawned on me which 'MJ' Quincy was referring to. Not *the* Michael Jackson? Michael Jackson was listening to *my* music. At that point I thought, if this is as far as the magic carpet ride goes, then we've arrived. I'm good. There's not much more I can ask for.

On my return from LA, I realised I needed my own space; somewhere I could call my own. So, I moved out of Paul's place and, between me, my mum and Colin, we came to the conclusion that, for the time being, I'd be better off living in a hotel rather than rushing to rent somewhere in London. I looked around and chose The Landmark in Marylebone. Moving in, I felt about as far away as I could imagine from my small bedroom on a council estate in Southampton.

It's funny. You can be staying in a place far from home in every respect, but you can still make it feel like home. I ended up making this hotel bedroom a more luxurious version of my room in Southampton – decks on the dressing table, vinyls under the desk, speakers wherever I wanted them. I can't deny that I liked the room service – fresh towels and linen on a more regular basis than back at home – but what I liked most was the feeling of containment in this small but perfectly formed space at the end of what were becoming crowded and full-on days.

I had to pinch myself; life had changed so much and so quickly. There was something going on all the time and life was getting so busy that, for the first time, I needed someone to help me out and, as if by magic, along came Patsy, who would be my PA for the next 13 years. Colin was now my manager; I even had a driver. Rows of fresh clothes and trainers were being sent to the hotel – these were hectic, high-octane times. What's not to like? It was so good, like some ongoing beautiful actualisation. I didn't want it to end. It was beyond my wildest dreams that this – writing songs, singing them, performing them – should be the thing that earned me a living. And beyond even those dreams, to see how my music resonated. I could see the way people were responding to my music – three nights sold out back to back at Wembley Arena – and things had moved on from the Notting Hill Carnival where no one would have believed me if I'd told them I was

Craig David. I was being recognised wherever I went, which was intoxicating.

There is a saying – 'act the part and you will become the part'. Well, since I'd come to London, I'd definitely had to act the part to become who I was now. There had been times since the success of 'Rewind' when I'd had to give myself a talking to that I'd got this, I could do this; that I had what it took to be this overnight success. I'd put on my beanie, I'd head out and I'd do my thing. Now that I *had* become the part, I was no longer acting.

WHAT'S CHANGED?

But maybe you get this – right from the moment that 'Rewind' was a success, at the back of my mind, there'd been this undercurrent, this low-grade humming: *You've fluked this. You might think people think you're good, but what do you know? What do they know? They'll soon see through you. They'll soon see you're just some kid from a council estate in Southampton. You've managed to get this past them and, if anything good comes from 'Fill Me In', they'll soon find out that you fluked that too.*

I now know that this was imposter syndrome – doubting my abilities and feeling like a fraud – which, over the next couple of decades, would stay with me. You might experience it yourself in your work or personal life. I had the classic attributes: I felt like a fake, everything that I'd done and any success I was having was down to luck or someone else and if anyone tried to give me praise, I'd tell them it was all 'no big deal'. On the outside, I was presenting as this confident young man, with nothing beyond his reach, nothing he couldn't sing or say. But inside I was unsure about pretty much everything other than my ability to hold a tune and freestyle.

On top of that, when I went back home to see my mum, the car I'd just bought and parked in the same car parking space we had used for 16 years, had the spoiler and bumper pulled off and left underneath during the night. I felt like a little piece of me had been pulled apart too. Why had someone done this? I felt responsible – that I hadn't been humble or grateful enough and I was no longer part of my own neighbourhood.

I wanted to still be the local lad loved by his friends and 'Craig David' could be the pop star. So I developed this defence mechanism, and that's when I started talking about myself – in interviews, to people in my team, to myself about myself – in the third person. It sounds a bit wonky, I know, but, trust me, it was the only way I had to process the drastic change in my life. As I saw it, there was me – the real me – and then there was a sort of Craig David brand, because that was easier for me to deal with. It was so hard to take in – I suddenly had the means for a new proper fancy car, travel and

I had this fear of being too big for my boots, of not being liked because I had things (I didn't deserve) that others didn't.

the best tables in restaurants. By splitting myself off, it was like I could still hold on to the piece of me I was comfortable with and had been for so long. I had this fear of being too big for my boots, of not being liked because I had things (I didn't deserve) that others didn't. Like J.Lo's 'Jenny from the Block', I wanted to hold on to being 'Craig from the Estate'.

Imposter syndrome embedded itself in me. Even when I had enough money to buy myself, and move into, a flat in Hampstead; even while I was releasing more albums – *Slicker than Your Average* in 2002 that included three singles, 'Hidden

Agenda', 'Rise & Fall' (a duet with Sting) and 'What's Your Flava?' (still my most-licenced song to this day, the video my homage to Willy Wonka) – I focused on 'not being found out', intent that no one would realise I was a young kid counting his blessings and waiting for his luck to run out.

I didn't have to wait long.

CHAPTER FIVE
Walking Away

Before the release of *Slicker Than Your Average*, the record label had already started to project – 'it's going to sell 10 million', 'the trajectory has to be higher than *Born To Do It*' – so when it actually sold 3.5 million copies, there was this feeling in the company that this was disappointing. I liked to always get things right, and so being told that 3.5 million was not a good thing was soul-destroying. Though I didn't really care about album sales – I was just happy to be there, making music, doing what I loved doing, literally living my dream – this feeling of failure chipped away at me. This was my first learning experience of being a product and being defined as a commodity that had to achieve certain targets. From it being me in my bedroom, there were now lots of cooks in the kitchen, each with their own opinion, and I began to equate my self-worth with other people's expectations of me.

I was making songs and they were connecting, but even if a track reached number four in the charts, it wasn't a Number One. And that started to matter to those around me. And then it became harder to produce what they wanted. The first albums came from my heart, they were me at my core; I was writing songs that came from who I was. Then, the more that was invested in me as an artist, as expectations grew, as I was busy touring or doing interviews all over the place, I was still supposed to conjure up what it was that I had before all this started, when I was more innocent, raw and pure. It was hard and I didn't always meet expectations, but I'm thankful for the moments that allowed me to dial down a bit and connect back to my heart, so that on *The Story Goes ...*, I included 'Let Her Go', which I wrote for my mum when my nan died. This song got me away from my head and the weight of expectation on me and back into my heart. And it connected with my fans and that made me know it was right.

On top of this growing sense of failure, came something that slowly started to unravel me and cut through the very heart of my music.

Bo' Selecta!, a Channel 4 'comedy' that ran from 2002 to 2009, had taken me as its main focus of derision and was a reflection, I guess, of my success at the time. Leigh Francis, the presenter, wrote and performed his show based on a line from one of my biggest songs and caricatured me – along with Michael Jackson, David Beckham, Mel B from The

Spice Girls and Trisha Goddard, as well as other well-known TV personalities – throughout. By relentlessly hitting on me and my music, thrusting this grotesque caricature which felt laser-focused on me, my worst imposter syndrome nightmares had come true.

'Rewind' had been so massive for me and that moment at the Notting Hill Carnival when I had watched as the crowd was so connected through the song, so happy and carefree and part of it, had helped me believe in my music. It's weird because it didn't really bother me that Leigh Francis was ridiculing me – that was no different to a *Spitting Image*-type caricature. I thought, *OK, this guy's a comedian and he's going to step on anyone to get where he needs to go, uncaring about who he hurts along the way. Each to their own, and it wouldn't be my bag*, but his endless hammering of 'Rewind' felt brutal. It was turning something that had been enjoyed and respected into a national joke. And because the show's title was a line from the song, it fell on me. Relentlessly. It was like he wanted to crush me.

Let me tell you, it all became too much for me. I was 21 years old when the series started and, in a heartbeat, I'd been reduced to a figure of ridicule, a kestrel on my shoulder, a colostomy bag at my side. He had me going around doing foolish things, being stupid and vain, and he made me say my own name in this sort of sing-song, inexplicably northern, voice that in real life came to haunt me. In the time that *Bo' Selecta!* was on Channel 4, with each season ratcheting up the 'fun', each painful show building on the last to imprint in the minds of the viewers how ridiculous I was, I had released three more albums – *The Story Goes ...*, *Trust Me* and my *Greatest Hits* – with each one, my belief in myself dropping, like the bassline.

I had written a song called 'Johnny' on *The Story Goes ...* – released in 2005 – which was about bullying, based on my experience in Year 8. A boy who was a couple of years above me would find me every day, push me up against a wall – any wall, it didn't matter where as long as there wasn't a teacher in sight – and demand money. I felt helpless to resist his threats; he was older, stronger and could have done more damage to me if I didn't hand over my change. I got off relatively lightly. There were kids around me who'd have someone from another school waiting outside the gates or at the bus stop for them.

'Johnny' resonated with a lot of listeners. It came from my heart and I realise now, of course, that it was my unconscious cry for help because of *Bo' Selecta!* and the bullying I was experiencing on a much larger and more public scale. I didn't put these two things together at the time – the lyrics describe a boy dragging his feet as he leaves for school, scared to face another day – but it can't be a coincidence that, so many years later, I was writing about this subject.

I had to save myself, without losing face. I had to escape the years of people shouting out my name in that horrible voice that had been imposed on me, the years of trying to do the 'right thing' by embracing the show, even at one point inviting Leigh Francis to sing 'Rewind' with me on stage at the Royal Albert Hall. I'd been advised to 'go with it' rather than speak out against what he was doing to me and while, at the time, that seemed to be the prevailing vibe, in my heart of hearts, I knew that I was not being true to myself. But I was young and impressionable, and I was constantly up against falling – a word I heard as 'failing' – record sales.

TIME TO PARTY

In 2010, I made the decision to move to Miami – partly to escape all this and partly driven by the idea that I could reinvent a polished new version of myself. While I'd publicly laughed *Bo' Selecta!* off, kept putting out records – in 2010, *Signed, Sealed, Delivered* (a covers album) – and not let it 'get to me', I knew that things weren't right within myself, though I wasn't yet anywhere *near* ready to confront what that show had done to me. I was on fragile ground and, in leaving the UK, I was turning away from all that was making my life miserable on the inside, while I was, despite being humiliated and shamed, having to appear all shiny and positive on the outside. I felt exposed and vulnerable and, while I played it as a desire to live the best life in the sunshine, unconsciously, I was running away from those feelings.

I felt exposed and vulnerable and I was running away from those feelings.

It had been a dream of mine to have a place in Miami since I'd first gone in 2001, when I was 20. 'Fill Me In' had been released and I'd been over to the US to perform. While I'd watched countless movies about Miami, I'd never actually been there or anywhere like it, and I fell in love the moment I left the airport. That ride over the Causeway past Star Island, past Fisher Island and over to South Beach ... it felt so good. The intensity of the heat and the light, and the welcome I received, made me feel great and, for a few years, I'd come back for New Year with my friend and guitarist, Fraser T Smith, to do acoustic sets across town and make a holiday of it. By this time, I was earning enough to be able to stay in some of the smartest hotels with great pools, spas, restaurants and bars.

Fast forward to my decision to buy a place out there. Fortunately for me, two things aligned: the pound was strong against the dollar and at the Mondrian – a place I had already come to love in LA – the condos were being redeveloped and sold. The hotel faces away from the beach, instead looking out over the bay and into the cityscape, and when the broker showed me around, I had my eye on one of the nice little apartments on the fifth floor. Just as we were leaving, he turned to me and said, 'You know what, I've got this place upstairs. It'll probably be beyond your price range, but while you're here you might as well see it.' (Yeah, that old chestnut.) So we got in the elevator and he pressed a button marked 'TS5' – Tower Suite 5, above the penthouse.

And when I walked out onto this huge, sun-filled balcony with the view of the bay and the city, it took my breath away and all I could think was: *I have to make this work.* So, I put my Hampstead flat on the market – this was a big step for me as I'd loved living there and, over the past few years, had made it feel like home – and collaborated with an interior designer to help me get the Miami apartment set up to accommodate my needs and taste. I love making my environment as comfortable and aesthetically pleasing as I can and it was important to me that I could put my own stamp on the empty shell of my new home. I also needed a studio and that took some time to sort out. Altogether it took about a year for my sale to go through and TS5 to be fitted out.

I wasn't taking much to Miami apart from clothes and a few possessions that meant something to me, like my collection of vinyls and old family photos. I put a lot of my furniture in storage, including my bed. I wasn't interested in selling them or giving them away because, somewhere deep down, I didn't think I was leaving London forever. I guess I didn't want to sever all my ties with the city I had grown to love, and this was one way of keeping a part of me still there.

On so many levels it was hard saying goodbye to my life in the UK. I knew I'd be back regularly and that those closest to me would make it out to Miami, but it did hit me that I was up and leaving. I'd recently allowed myself the luxury of a housekeeper to help run things around the flat for me and I found it very hard to say goodbye to her. Gina had arrived like an angel from heaven and, while she gave me space to do my own thing and I was respectful of her autonomy around the place, I loved her serenity and wisdom and unexpected humour – the way she made me laugh until tears ran down my cheeks. Before I left, I made sure she knew that if she was around when I came back to London, there was always a place for her in my home.

But I knew that I couldn't stay around and take much more of the *Bo' Selecta!* banter, parts of me dying inside every time someone called out my name in that sing-song way. As far as I was concerned, I was heading to a new life, a new iteration of myself, so off I flew to the life I'd seen in the movies and wanted to be a part of.

For a long time, Miami was fresh and exciting, and I loved it. My home was stunning, with spectacular views and interiors I could never have dreamed of, and the lifestyle was something else. There was the bright, hot, yellow sunshine, those blue skies, the shimmering heat. There was the endless, rolling sound of the sea, the taste of the salty air that I loved. There was the nightlife – privileged entry to restaurants that were so exclusive they didn't even have menus, nightclubs where the social life was on fire – and the thrilling possibility of finding a girl to take home and make love to.

And I threw myself into it all. I looked around every day and saw the beauty in the sculpted bodies around me, the sheen of glamour along the boardwalk and in the restaurants and clubs. There was this weird combination of people around me knowing exactly who I was and wanting me to be part of their scene, while at the same time this relief of anonymity, as *Bo' Selecta!* was not on anyone's radar. It was such a vibe in those early days. I couldn't believe my luck at my change in lifestyle.

Everything in Miami was about appearance – how you looked, what shape you were in, body, body, body. In bed; out of bed; on the beach; along the boardwalk; by the pool; in the clubs … If you were going to be seen, it was through the veil of your body.

And once you were seen, there was no slacking – you could just as quickly be unseen. So, something told me I needed to get with the programme. I guess my subconscious was telling me I needed to fit in, to not put myself in any danger of standing out or, worse than that, being ridiculed.

SLICKER THAN YOUR AVERAGE

There's working out and there's working out, and I soon found that working out in Miami took muscle-work to a different level. It wasn't hard – everyone around me was at it, seeking some sort of elixir through extreme physical punishment. I became fixated on serious bodybuilding too, honing and toning obsessively, monitoring everything I ate, spending hours training. Every day, I'd go to the gym and work out until I had no more to give, believing I was my most healthy, most strong, most in control of my body.

This suited me. I'd been mindful of my body for a long time; obsessed, even. Back when I'd started working out at around the age of 13 in an attempt to shed the pounds, I'd picked up an interest in how I could *sculpt* my body. I couldn't afford a trainer or anything, so I just did whatever pushed me to the extreme. I'd pick up weights that were far too heavy for my young body and throw them around until it hurt. If I was out of breath or I finished a session at the limits of endurance, I thought I was doing a great job. As it turns out, I wasn't. As a result of punching above my weight, my muscles grew too quickly, and I've still got the stretch marks on my shoulders to prove it. In Miami, I went even further and, together with hardly eating anything, for a while the adrenalin of such fierce discipline was like some sort of drug and I was on a perpetual high.

Before long, I was looking and feeling in peak condition, had fallen in with a crowd that knew how to party and I had a great apartment. What better, then, than to combine all three and throw my place open to all and sundry, keeping the drinks flowing and the music pumping. I was not a fan of the red rope thing in the nightclubs I was going to; it felt elitist – you could only cross into certain spaces if you were rich enough, famous enough or hot enough. So, opening my apartment to whoever, no questions asked on income or fame or looks, made me feel as if I was doing something fresh.

This called for what I knew best and felt most comfortable doing – an iteration of my musical self, that hadn't, so far, become a national joke. Mixing, DJing, ad-libbing, emcee-ing, singing over tracks – it was second nature to me. And it brought me an adoring crowd, plenty of willing Floridians happy to flood into my apartment on Friday and Saturday nights for free pre-party drinks and food, me on the decks bringing the R&B, garage and bashment vibes, just like back in my PCRS 105.3 days.

I couldn't get enough of all these people around me, there because of my music (and possibly the fountain of tequila too). I was being seen, I was doing what I loved and it made me feel safe, transported back to my bedroom in Southampton while contained in this fancy high-rise in Miami – my safe space. Word soon got around and these evenings – which I called TS5 after the location of my apartment – seemed to catch the

Miami vibe. Colin also loved what I was creating every time I uploaded a set from the party to my SoundCloud account and he had even got radio stations back home so interested that they, too, started airing it. Before I knew it, we had thousands of listeners tuning in from across the world.

If I'd taken more than an occasional moment to pause, I might have predicted what was coming, but there was no sustained pausing back then. The good-time vibes continued to give and, mostly, I wasn't looking back. I was still coming to the UK three or four times a year, writing songs with the Backstreet Boys, doing some TS5 tours and catching up with friends and family, and Colin and my team, sometimes a flash of longing to be home sparking briefly. But when I took part in the 2011 Big Red Nose Desert Trek – a bunch of us, including Lorraine Kelly, Dermot O'Leary, Nadia Sawalha and Olly Murs, raising awareness of and money for those with sight loss – there was a moment when my sense of where I really belonged almost floored me.

After the initial excitement of taking off for our 100-kilometre trek through Kenya's Kaisut desert in temperatures of 50 degrees, the reality of our task hit us. It was on about the third day that we began to suffer – stomach bugs, mouth ulcers, fatigue, blisters … you name it. We had sat down to rest when I noticed that Lorraine had removed herself from the group and was sitting alone. She looked a bit down, so I went over to check she was OK.

'I'm trying Craig,' she told me. 'I'm really trying, but I'm missing home so much. And my feet hurt and I'm not sure I am going to make it.'

We had already bonded as a group, but we were still discovering things about each other, so as I gently massaged her feet to help relieve the swelling, I asked her to tell me more about where she came from, her husband, Steve, and her daughter, Rosie. As she brought them to life for me, I could feel her separation from them so powerfully, it was as if it were a physical thing. And as I experienced her profound sense of belonging – to people, to a place – I felt a weight of longing, wishing that I, too, had these sorts of anchors back home, this deep sense of love and being rooted.

I felt a weight of longing, wishing that I, too, had this deep sense of love and being rooted.

While this brought things to the surface for me, this feeling of wanting to return to the UK was still a little premature and I wasn't quite ready to make the plunge back overseas. However, Lorraine always made that bridge feel available, an extended invitation to come back when I was ready, connected with an invisible cord, an energetic bond made in Kenya. She would always be there for me over the years that followed, constantly talking me up and defending my corner, while becoming a guardian angel I didn't even know I had.

But, even though life in Miami, for the moment, was still vibrating with enough sunshine and good times to hold me at bay, deep down, maybe even somewhere nearer the surface than I thought, something wasn't right. I could feel myself out of alignment. I only had to look at my music to realise something was up. Despite going to the expense and trouble of installing a state-of-the-art studio in my apartment, I'd hardly gone in it and, in the years I'd been in Miami, I hadn't written anything I was pleased with or could imagine recording.

Moving to Miami had been a big thing and I'd assured Colin that I'd be working hard out there, putting in the hours, sending songs backwards and forwards to the team. But from the moment the studio was set up, rather than writing or recording anything, I'd kind of *visit* it, popping in on my way from the kitchen, playing a bit of R&B, then walking out onto the terrace, where I'd slap on a bit of lotion, lie on a lounger and soak up the sun. It's Miami, I'd say to myself. It's hot. I'll enjoy the day, live in the moment. Sort of freestyle-YOLO.

As I'd settle down in the sun, I'd reassure myself that I'd pick it back up in the early evening before going out. But then early evening came and I'd get a call from friends telling me someone was in town, we were meeting at this or that restaurant and going on to this or that club. And I'd get this FOMO, go back into the apartment, bypassing the studio, take a shower, have a drink, put on some fresh clothes and leave. A few more drinks later, my throat would feel dry and I'd think, the falsetto won't be happening, so tomorrow I'll rest my voice a bit … and then when I was up mid-morning the next day, I'd go into the studio, play some R&B to get me in the mood, see the sun, slide open the balcony door and … you get the picture.

So, the music wasn't happening in the usual way. And the bodybuilding regime, well, that was going hyper. I hit a point where my body fat got down so low that I proudly took a 'bodpod' test at the University of Miami to measure the level. Just so you know, the average for a man is between 18 and 24 per cent. When I came out of the pod and the guy told me mine was 4.5 per cent, I was so pumped, I hit the air with my fist and told him, as I left, that I was working on getting it down more. It was only later, when I went online and read that, below 4 per cent, there's a danger of your organs shutting down, that I realised why he wasn't quite as impressed as I'd expected.

Now, of course, looking back at the photos I posted on social media at the time, I can see just how horrifically skeletal I looked. People were asking me, 'Man, you OK?' Even friends in the body-perfect Florida paradise were alarmed, telling me straight up that I looked gaunt.

At first, I couldn't see it. I felt great. I could feel the endorphins, I could feel the adrenalin. I could take on the world. I barely looked at my face or my body as a whole. Instead, I'd be honing in on one part of me and thinking, *I need to work on that*. I was so attuned to the levels of fat in my body, that if I sensed or saw a millimetre creeping back, I'd go down hard on it, over and over, and change what I was eating – until it was gone.

It's not like my body wasn't protesting. If I'd been listening to it or was attuned to what I was feeling, then I'd have heard it. Since starting this unforgiving regime, I'd had all sorts of physical problems, including a sharp, intermittent pain in my back that wouldn't go away. I'd have heard the creaks, felt those twinges, as more than inconveniences to be ignored, and listened in. Talk about tuning out what my body was trying to tell me – as far off-key as I could have been.

I truly believed my body was a machine. That it was somehow separate from my mind and spirit. That if I could appear a certain way, achieve a certain look, keep working harder and pushing my body harder, it would make me feel complete. And then, because Instagram was becoming a big thing, I would post pictures of my body – me in the gym, me out for a run, me flexing. I needed the approval, the likes. I needed to be able to post a better picture than the person I thought looked better than me.

Looking back, I realise that I was in a state of needing total control over my body; to be seen for who I was; to get as far away physically from the Craig David who everyone thought wore a colostomy bag and had a great big rubber face and gigantic, distorted chin. But, back then, I didn't have that level of self-awareness and was mostly in denial that the show had affected me so deeply. I was in the thick of some sort of toxic mixture of acceptance and denial, hijacked mentally and physically by *Bo' Selecta!*, my confidence hacked away by the relentless parodying.

I realise now that I had become just another grotesque embodiment of who I wasn't. And while the focus may have shifted away from the puppet to this new physicality, I still wasn't being seen, first and foremost by myself, for who I really was or had been back in the days when everything was flowing – those faraway days of 'Rewind' and 'Fill Me In', when I felt as if I were riding the crest of the wave over and over, never coming anywhere near the shore.

Even if I thought at the time – which I so mistakenly did – that I had reached some kind of physical perfection, had trained so hard that I'd achieved something no one could take away from me, subconsciously, I knew that things were very wonky. And even though I was part of the pantomime, I was beginning to see it for what it was. The more I saw myself, the more disturbed I became by how far I'd come from being healthy and looking good, and I knew that I needed to pull back from this ridiculous training and restricted eating and realign, both internally and externally.

It was the same with the TS5 parties. The shine was wearing off. I began to dread the onslaught, the invasion of my apartment that ended in it looking like it had been trashed. One evening, I looked around from my decks and could only see a swaying, swirling bunch of strangers. I'd overheard people complaining about the range of drinks and the type of food, and more and more were using it as a pre-party tank-up before going on to clubs. By this time, I'd been on tour with TS5, and I'd created something successful and popular. So, why was I still throwing open my doors, still trying to be Mr Popular?

Being aware that things were going wonky was the first step. The second was reading the signs around me and responding to what was going on. And that led to a series of moments that made me recalibrate, big time.

LOUDER THAN WORDS

I had dialled down my bodybuilding when I'd heard and seen what everyone around me, including Colin, was telling me – that I looked ill, the lines on my face making me look old. But I was still convinced that what I looked like on the outside counted. So, when I was invited to a dinner some friends of mine were hosting downtown and I noticed this one guy walk in, two things struck me. The first was that he had this stunning woman with him and the second was that he had an enormous pot belly. In the looks-obsessed, perfect-body world that I was inhabiting, this was unusual – an overweight man with a good-looking woman. So, I automatically assumed – and may I be struck down now for such unconscious thinking – he was some kind of sugar daddy and she must be in it for the money.

Don't get me started on how terrible a judgement that was, but, back then, in that plush, lush Miami restaurant, that was my thinking. After everyone was settled in their places, this guy stood up and began to tell a story, taking us on a journey, an emotional rollercoaster, leaving us dangling and then bringing us back down to earth again. And he spoke along this table as if he were talking to each of us personally. I felt like I knew him. He had us all mesmerised, he had us all bellyaching with laughter and I then understood exactly why this girl was with him. In telling this story, in engaging us all with his inclusive words and embracing vibe, it was like we were all falling in love with him. He may not have looked as toned and honed as everyone else. He may not have been body-perfect. But he seemed at ease with who he was; he had accepted who he was, on the inside and outside, and had embraced it. He didn't need any fancy fireworks to be seen. It came from a place within him.

My bodybuilding thing was a joke – what was I working towards? Sure, look good, feel good, exercise well and eat healthily. But I wasn't training to be a professional body-builder. This wonky *obsession* had taken over my life and I had believed that how I looked was what mattered above all else. But until I accepted myself on the inside, I was never going to be accepted on the outside. Nothing made me see that more clearly than meeting this charismatic guy.

Feeling like I wanted so desperately to spend more time in that kind of company, especially how I felt so seen by him, crystallised my awareness of feeling lost and alone. It was Christmas 2014 and my body felt depleted and shattered, my sofas and walls had been mashed by the crowd that shoved itself into my living room, and even my music, which had been my biggest saviour and protection up until this point, was now not happening.

How had I got to this point? Why had I been so keen to be seen and, in the process, lost some of the values that nourished me? Because that imposter syndrome that I had felt in the very early days was still lurking somewhere in the shadows; because I had been shattered by the dismantling of my happiest 'Rewind' self – and that combination doubled down on how, deep down, I still felt that I wasn't worthy and that

I needed to find new ways to prove to everyone that I was. I had tried to run away to seek out some sort of false paradise in Miami, embracing its culture of looking good, even if that meant falling apart inside.

CHAPTER SIX
Fast Cars

The second moment when I realised that my life was out of alignment – that I was veering too far from who I was – happened, believe it or not, when I was sitting in a red Ferrari F430 outside Prime 112, a fancy restaurant in Miami. It was midnight, I'd just had a beautiful meal with friends and was about to head to a club with my date for the night.

Every time I got behind that wheel, it felt dreamy and dream-like. As a young boy back in Southampton, after music and hi-fi equipment, there was nothing I enjoyed more than hitting up the local arcade and playing my favourite racing game *OutRun*. I'd save up my pound coins and, after school, go down to the local marina where the arcade was, make myself comfortable in the low-down driver's seat and play until I'd run out of money. As soon as I pushed that start button, it was *me* sitting in that open-top red Ferrari, *my* arm around the girl, *me* hurtling past the palm trees, along the wide, sunny, coastal roads, heroically outmanoeuvring all the traffic.

And now, here I was, all these years later in Miami, sitting in my own Ferrari with my date by my side with palm trees lining the streets. I mean talk about manifesting the full *OutRun* experience – the marina had now been replaced with Miami Beach and the pound coin slot was now a shiny stereo head unit loaded with all my favourite R&B tunes.

AWKWARD

Like I did every time I sat behind the wheel, I shook away my disbelief and reached for the start button on the steering wheel, excited to hear that roar of the 500-horsepower engine. It was a sticky-hot Miami night and I needed to get the engine up and running quick and the air conditioning on. But, as I pressed the start button, I heard this strange *juh-juh-juh* noise from the engine. I tried again: *juh-juh-juh*. No good. I was starting to sweat. I tried again a few more times, nervously turning to smile at my date. I knew I had to think on my feet to pre-empt her getting too hot and agitated as I couldn't even open the windows, so I suggested she jump in the cab with my friends, reassuring her I'd meet them at the club. It was so uncomfortable in the car that she didn't take too much persuading.

By now, other diners had crowded around to take a look at the car and, as I tried to start it again, the front headlights were doing some bizarre flashing number every time I pressed the start button. The *juh-juh-juh* was percussive and menacing and I thought, *I've got to stop turning this engine over as I'm gonna mash the electrics.* I had to take some action. So I called Brett, the guy who'd sold me the car. I could always count on him when I had car trouble and he picked up straightaway.

'Brett,' I said, 'I'm outside Prime 112, in the car and the battery's gone; it won't turn on man. I feel like a joker and I'm on this date. This ain't a good look bro and I want to get to the club before she blows cold and thinks I'm not pitching up.'

Brett was always super calm. 'Craig,' he said, 'there's a reset procedure and all you have to do is press the ignition button ten times, open the door ten times, and this will sort it. It's not the battery as that's brand new.'

Feeling like I was in an Ashton Kutcher *Punk'd* sketch, waiting for the lights and video cameras to pop out at any moment, I proceeded to follow Brett's pantomime reset procedure. But ten ignition presses and open–shut–open door routines later, with the car flashing like a Christmas tree, the *juh-juh-juh* sound of the engine had not gone away. By now, all the waiters and kitchen staff were clocking off and even the valet guy had gone home. I called Brett back. Super calm still, he apologised profusely and said he'd send a flatbed tow truck that would get to me within the hour.

As the minutes ticked down ever so slowly, the restaurant now fully closed and the area completely deserted, I thought I might as well jump out of the car and at least get some air. But just as I was about to open the door, the loudest clap of thunder hit and the heavens opened. FML. So I just sat there, rain pouring down outside, sweat soaking through my shirt inside, stressed and agitated as the minutes ticked down like an old clock that hadn't been wound. An hour passed by, no tow truck. Another half-hour and I finally gave up with the idea of meeting up with my date and friends, so I texted her: *'Not looking good for making it to the club tonight – my bad, the car's just not having it.'* A few minutes later she texted back: *'No worries. Catch you soon.'*

Now feeling slightly less anxious that I needed to get somewhere and knowing the night was officially a write-off, I sat in a kind of trance gazing out at the rain pouring down the windscreen, almost accepting I could be sitting in this steaming box of steel and leather till morning, and it was then, in this moment of acceptance, that I was struck, for the first time, by the brilliance of the yellow badge in the middle of the steering wheel with the black horse of the Ferrari embossed on it.

And as I stared at it, it was as if every thought of the pear-shaped evening disappeared. I examined the stitching, giving it my real, undivided attention, looking next at the detail on the dashboard and the little F430 ensign, the cream and leather seats, and the gleaming, plush interior. I thought about the way that car had been designed and engineered, the way the doors opened, the glide and slide of it on the road, and I felt this surge of emotion come over me. I felt like I'd literally – and this isn't adding any sauce or spice to hype this up – gone from being in my car to being in that seat in *OutRun* back in the arcade in Southampton. It was the most real out-of-body experience I'd ever had.

As quickly as I was out-of-body, I was back in the present, back in this broken-down real Ferrari, outside an actual restaurant in Miami and I started to cry. Key moments of my life flashed past me – my bedroom back in Southampton; my nan's stews; my Studio 100 hi-fi; going up to London with my mum to buy vinyls; the guys sitting outside Bego's; my nose pressed against Richer Sound's window.

And I had this overwhelming feeling of gratitude. Waves and waves of appreciation for the care and love I'd been given. Waves and waves of appreciation for the excitement that had literally run through my veins as I did my first DJ set at my dad's club. Waves and waves of appreciation for the innocent pleasure *OutRun* had given me, and a tsunami of appreciation for all the chances I'd taken and the spaces in which I'd had to dream.

I sat there with tears pouring down my cheeks, but also with this immense sense of clarity that here I was, that boy from Southampton, 'living the dream', here and now, and that was all I needed to know. This sense of peace descended and flooded through me, and I stopped crying and sat there, still, patient and calm. When the tow truck arrived 45 minutes later, I was ready and thankful when I was dropped home. I'd experienced something back on that tarmac that would impact the next phase of my life.

Later, surrounded by the whitewashed walls of my luxurious apartment, I reflected on why it had meant so much to me to have experienced that profound moment of connection to my childhood, to my bedroom, to the uncomplicated happiness of playing *OutRun* – to the time, I guess, when I was at my happiest and that was now a thing of the past. That was the second moment when I realised that my life was out of kilter. I was so far from the boy in the arcade, the true me, that I had to find some way back.

I was so far from the
boy in the arcade, the
true me, that I had to
find some way back.

WHO YOU ARE

Being reflective wasn't something I was used to – my life was fast, sometimes flashing by so quickly I didn't have time to take it all in. But, from this point. I started to piece things together and, inevitably, I thought back to who I was and where I'd come from.

One minute I'd been DJing at the under-18s 'What You Want (What You Need)' club night in Southampton and the next thing I was performing in nightclubs all over London, with the Artful Dodger and then on my own. From there, it had all taken off so quickly: a Number One album with *Born To Do It*; industry and chart awards; travelling across the world; and all these young guys asking for the same hairstyle and beard as me, even my trademark beanie. And because it all happened so fast, I didn't know how to quantify it, how to cope with, manage or internalise it. All I knew at the time was that I had to push down any feelings of insecurity – feelings that someone in the record company would think I was a one-hit wonder, that I was too young, too inexperienced, not cool enough, not worldly enough. Not enough-enough.

And so, I kept it all positive on the outside – my smile, my attitude, my vibe – and it seemed to work. Before long, I realised that if I kept on smiling, kept on saying yes and kept on being up for everything, whether or not it was in my best interest, no one would see me for the imposter I really was.

Being positive was my mask. And when I was feeling not so positive somewhere inside, I squashed it. My internal beat was telling me that negative thinking was not OK, that even in order to project an image of success, I needed to feel and be at my best all the time.

What I came to see was that before I 'made it', being positive – or maybe just innocent – most definitely hadn't been a conscious thing. It wasn't like I had to *make* myself smile, *make* myself available, *make* myself turn up. It was just how I was. It came from the pure excitement of making music. It came from a place of freedom – what did I have to lose? I had everything to gain by trying, by taking a leap of faith because, if I didn't, I'd never know. And this was all before I was 17, so every opportunity seemed exciting, unreal and enticing.

Running alongside my relentless positivity of always saying yes, always showing up, always bringing the good vibes to the table, had been this overwhelming need to be liked, to please everyone around me. And I'd said yes, always shown up smiling, empathising with people's needs and requests, *irrespective of how I was feeling or whether or not I actually wanted to do something.* Many times, so many times now I thought about it, I hadn't wanted to say yes, I hadn't wanted to show up, I hadn't wanted to do the things I'd been asked to do. I felt like Jim Carrey in the movie *Yes Man*, in which his character, Carl, after attending a motivational session, promises to say yes to every invite, request or opportunity that comes his way.

Always saying 'yes' and exuding positivity was my way of striving for that need for social approval.

There's no way to sugar-coat this: I was your classic people-pleaser. I wanted everyone to enjoy themselves; even if I wasn't, even if they weren't. I wanted everyone to have a good time; even if I wasn't, even if they weren't. I never wanted to say no, even when I couldn't say yes. I had a deep-rooted fear that, if I said no or didn't make the effort, other people would not like me, even though I knew not everyone would like me anyway. Gaps, silences, awkwardness were all no-gos in my book – I wanted to fill them in, I wanted to cover them up so that no one felt uncomfortable or that the good vibes were wonky.

This was a moment of absolute clarity for me. I'd been sitting in my dream car, in Miami, with all the things that I thought would give me joy, yet I was lacking that authenticity of just being enough without all the bells and whistles. Always saying 'yes' and exuding positivity was my way of striving for that need for social approval. But, in reality, I was actually lacking those deeper connections – both in love and friend-ships – that I yearned for, those meaningful relationships that nourish the soul. I realised in that moment that I had built a life that wasn't really me.

CHAPTER SEVEN
Talk to Me

My experience of relationships after my teenage years was pretty wonky. Let's be honest, finding fame at 18 may seem like any kids' dream, but it doesn't make finding real love – or true friendship – simple. When life took off in ways I'd never dreamed of, I leaned into the multitude of opportunities that came my way, without pausing to consider what they were doing to my life and my relationships. I was travelling all over the place, doing photo shoots here, there and everywhere, getting VIP treatment at clubs and restaurants, and meeting beautiful women all the time. This is not an average teenager's experience of dating. At the time, I didn't even consider that this was not normal or that it might be reconfiguring my idea of relationships, dating and love – every day was exciting and full of new people to get to know, to vibe off. It was really easy to put myself out there, with my new-found confidence and success, and have physical relationships while avoiding emotional connections completely – and, with that, avoiding all risk of hurt or rejection.

If the woman I was dating tried to get me to open up, to go deeper, to get closer than the physical, I instantly became uncomfortable and walked away. I reasoned that I didn't need to have my heart broken again. I didn't want to ever feel what I felt after going to Nicky's house. I wanted to keep myself focused on my music, the 'safe' love of my life. I can honestly say that I have missed out on so many beautiful opportunities of deep relationships because every time a woman has ever wanted to get closer to me, was prepared to go that extra mile and love me, I automatically shut down. Not only did I remain closed off, but I didn't allow myself to give any signs of longer term commitment so that wonderful, beautiful women – beautiful in hearts, minds and souls – would, in the end, for their own self-preservation, have to walk away from me too.

I wanted to keep myself focused on my music, the 'safe' love of my life.

And I was also so wary of the press at that time. If there wasn't endless speculation about why I wasn't dating, if I was with a woman, we'd be snapped and she'd be subjected to some sort of scrutiny into her private life too.

My experience, I can see, is quite extreme and specific to my life circumstances, but I suspect I might not be the only one closed off to something so important as love. Love is scary, it makes you vulnerable, it hurts, it can break you down, it can test you, it can damage your ability to trust others. And yet, it is one of the most important and wonderful parts of being human.

PERSONAL

I'd made a lot of friends in Miami and was never short of an invitation to lunch, to supper, for a drink, to a club. I had endless dates, I was rarely alone and then there were all the people who came to my place for my weekly TS5 sets. This was Miami – sunshine, sex and sushi – and the vibe was chilled and frantic and, somehow, it worked. But even though there were people around me all the time, I was coming to see that what I missed was close friends and my family, who I had left back in London.

It seemed that no sooner had I realised what I'd been missing, it was as if the universe heard my call for this more authentic connection and started to place people around me for me to meet. One morning, while I was lifting weights in the gym, I got talking to Grant, a personal trainer who I'd seen in the gym many times before, putting different clients through their paces. I knew that he knew who I was, and was grateful that he'd never tried to crack the leave-me-alone protective shell that vibrated off me when I was in the gym.

I was busy heaving weights on the bench press and, when I slammed them down, he suggested I try lifting lighter ones while using one of those large exercise balls as a bench. He gave me some lighter weights and watched as I rolled about all over the place, barely able to stay on the ball.

I said, 'Woah, I can't do this.'

He smiled and said, 'I know you go hard, but with a tweak here and there you could do it more safely and smarter too.'

I decided in that moment to ask for help and booked a PT session with him there and then. That was the beginning of what became a close friendship that continues to this day – fast forward through many gym sessions and weekly excursions to get cheesecake, to me singing at his wedding to his beautiful wife Corinne. Once I became friends with Grant, I found myself opening up to more people around me.

For example, the gym was usually mostly empty and, while I was training, I'd bring in a little hi-fi and play some R&B and throwback hip-hop, and I'd push weights and it was all good vibes. Quite often, though, a woman would come in and, as soon as she heard my music, she'd get this disgruntled look on her face and ask me or Grant, in a way that meant we were not to mess with her, to turn the music down. Then she'd put on her headphones and get on the treadmill and not engage with us in any way. This just caned our whole vibe, but it wasn't my private space, so we'd notch it down a few.

This went on for a couple of months and I noticed that she was always there when I was and, because I never saw her anywhere else in the building – at the pool, in one of the communal areas – I wondered where she was coming in from. Something inside was nagging me to get to the bottom of it.

One day, before she went on autopilot with the turn-the-music-down thing, I made sure I had no music on and just said, 'Hi, I'm Craig. We're in here the whole time together and I don't even know your name.'

She looked at me and said, 'Well, my name is Jill.'

I continued, 'Jill, I'm really sorry when we play the music loud. Me and Grant get into our groove and get a bit overexcited. How are you?'

And it was like this magic thing happened. All of a sudden, her veil dropped, her face softened and she smiled. 'I'm pretty good thanks,' she replied.

She thanked me for turning the music down and explained that she came to the gym to walk in order to stave off the symptoms of multiple sclerosis (MS). She told me, 'I have to get into my zone and, because I listen to my audiobooks in here, I find it hard when your music is playing so loud over the top.'

Fair enough. Our music was pretty loud and definitely more on the pumping weights side, not exactly the sound you'd want to hear smashing over the top of a good audiobook. When I found out about her MS, I immediately wanted to do all we could to make her gym sessions calm – to give her the right vibes so she could do all the exercise she needed. After that, whenever we were in the gym at the same time, we turned off our music and also started to talk more.

It turned out that Jill lived in the Mondrian too and we had lunch a bunch of times and talked about life. She was wise and dignified and could see things about life more clearly than me. We formed this friendship which felt nourishing and meaningful, symbiotic and caring. Somehow, she could tell I was struggling, even though on the surface my life seemed so silky smooth, so she gently put me on to Brené Brown's *The Power of Vulnerability* and suggested I download the audiobook and listen to it through my headphones. I liked the sound of that, having lived a lot of my best life through my headphones, so I leaned in.

That evening for my cardio session, I chose to take up Jill's advice and go for a slow jog on the boardwalk and listen to her recommendation. The sun was just setting, caressing the sky in a way that made it shimmer in beautiful shades of pink, the air fresh and the foliage lush and green. I put on my

If we open up
emotionally and
feel the pain of life,
this will allow us to
also feel the joys.

headphones, inhaled all the good vibes, got in my zone and pressed 'play'. As Brené spoke, I felt a deep sense of connection to her and it seemed that her words sparked something inside of me that felt familiar. Being vulnerable, she told me through my headphones, doesn't mean you're weak. It is, in fact, the *only* way to show strength, bravery and courage, and there isn't a single act of courage that doesn't involve vulnerability. To accept vulnerability in life, she says, does not result in the possibility of pain, but the guarantee of it. If we open up emotionally and feel the pain of life, this will allow us to also feel the joys.

Wow. This resonated with me so deeply. I even pulled up on the side of the boardwalk to rewind it, just so I could hear it again. It was like she was saying what I'd felt inside for so long – I'd just never heard anyone express it as clearly as she did. This was the start of something big, life-enhancing and life-changing, opening me up to the possibility of gaining insight from those who knew what they were talking about, outsiders who didn't know the specifics of my life, but who spoke in ways that felt relevant to the things I was experiencing and feeling. I began to listen carefully, constantly repeating sections so they could settle deep in me and I could think about how to apply what I was hearing.

Running along the boardwalk in the Miami sunshine became a little different – I'd still have my headphones on, but instead of thumping away to the latest hip-hop banger, I was alive to the beat of the spoken word. It made me smile as I exchanged thumbs-ups with other runners, who must have thought I was listening to some throwback Biggie the way I was bouncing off the wooden slats. If only they knew what was driving me onwards, stirring me to see my surroundings – and my own situation – in a different light.

FOCUS

I don't know if you find this, but sometimes, when you dip your toe in the water and it's not as hot or cold as you expected, it's actually quite pleasant – not just pleasant, but satisfying – and gives you a warm feeling. You then want to go back for more, expand your experiences and start to face the things that have made your world shift on its axis, knocking you out of alignment and on a trajectory you don't want to be on. Once you see where you're off, you can then make the conscious decision to get back on track.

Listening to Brené Brown made me curious and, before long, I was exploring different teachers – both practical and spiritual. I began to drill down into the insights of Belinda Womack, whose teachings focus on the awakening of our innate spiritual power, harnessing it to rebuild our self-esteem; Eckhart Tolle, who emphasises the power and meaning of being in the moment, the allure of *now*; and Shakti Gawain who taught me the process of creative visualisation. In each of their own ways, these teachers – these guiding lights – gave me the foundations of the solace and comfort I was seeking.

I also came to realise that being vulnerable was actually the doorway to true courage and that it was OK to not immediately see a solution; and that by just knowing that others are there for us – whether that's a family member, a friend or a professional – we can turn down the volume of our worries if we just reach out.

With this new-found insight, along with my connections to Grant and Jill, I was preparing myself for a massive reboot.

You see, for a while, moving to Miami and escaping the UK worked. I was healed and repaired by the sun on some level and by the anonymity I had there – no one shouted out my name to me in the street in that ridiculous sing-song voice and the papers weren't out for headlines. Inviting people into my apartment for music and drinks before the nightclubs revved up, being the host with the most and bringing good energy into my orbit was my definition of keeping things positive and fresh. It fitted with the Florida vibe I'd created for myself – the excesses that seemed more allowable in America than in the UK.

But by making my life in Miami big, bright and brash – and, don't get me wrong, a lot of it was easy and fun and I'd never change it – I'd allowed myself to be seduced by the on-show lifestyle, attempting to be seen through reinvention and surface things, like the way I looked and how many parties I could throw. I'd come to a place where no one was looking underneath the muscle-clad surface at my soul. Gradually, though, that life became unsustainable and I could now see how wonky things had become. I was the people-pleaser, Mr Positive, the one always saying yes, masking my feelings even from myself. Always pushing forward to find happiness, when the happiest I had ever been was in the past as a kid with lots of dreams, my music flowing through my veins.

As I slowly found the courage to face myself, I had this uncomfortable feeling that everything I was doing was an attempt – conscious and unconscious – to connect me to others and, more significantly, to try to get back to the me of the Notting Hill 'Rewind' moment, to the me who knew who I was, but who had been taken down, viciously and from nowhere, by a grotesque parody. Here I was, in the Sunshine State, the shiniest version of my shiny self, and I was still deeply lonely and unhappy.

I finally realised that I really needed meaningful relationships and the grounding of my family around me. Being cramped up in VIP areas of clubs, spilling drinks on myself, wasn't cutting it anymore. It was time to make some changes.

I was the people-pleaser, Mr Positive, the one always saying yes, masking my feelings even from myself.

CHAPTER EIGHT
Rise and Fall

Since moving to Miami in 2010, I'd kept the lines of connection open between my life there and my life back in London and Southampton. Colin was always there for me, but it seemed that even he couldn't get me fully back on my musical track. Always one step ahead and knowing what was good for me, in 2014 on one of his visits to Miami, he had introduced me to Evan Lamberg, President of the Universal Music Publishing Group. You know how sometimes you like someone the moment you meet them? Well, that was the case instantly – the second he walked into my apartment, Evan was open and warm and he put me at ease. We bonded straight away, not initially through our love of music, but because, spotting my generously portioned bowls of chocolate across the room, he pointed to them, smiled a deep childhood smile and told me that the vibe reminded him of his favourite movie, *Charlie and the Chocolate Factory*.

If he didn't have me at that, the time he subsequently took with me, the care and compassion he showed for what I wasn't even seeing myself, was something I will always be grateful for. My music candle may have been dimly lit at the time, but he saw the flame. He slowly encouraged me to reconnect to what had always been in there and, when he took a risk, signing me to Universal, telling me that the music 'would come good', I began to see myself in a different light. If my music, or lack of it, was still resonating out there for someone as connected as Evan, then it was down to me to bring it back to life.

When I came back to the UK, I either stayed with my mum or in London, at the Heathrow Airport Sofitel, which I loved for its easy access, especially when, in 2015, I found myself popping over two or three times a month. Evan would make regular stops whenever he was in town for meetings and, even though he could have stayed at any swanky hotel in London, he'd always insist on making it easier for me by booking a room at the Sofitel and making time for his golden-ticket friend to catch up on life, music and, obviously, our favourite movie.

Being back in the UK, I could feel something pulling me back and I knew in my heart of hearts that I needed to come home, that Miami had repaired me as much as it could – it had given me sunshine, distance and distraction in the form of fast cars. I hadn't been taunted by people calling out my name, asking me foolish questions about a kestrel or feeling bullied by the colostomy bag jibes that *Bo' Selecta!* had tried to make acceptable. And coming back home over the years since the show had come off-air in 2009, people here seemed to have forgotten about it and moved on, some TS5 fans too young to have ever even watched it. The air felt clearer and, when I performed 'Rewind', the crowd knew exactly what to do and loved it, feeling the energy and vibe, just like we all did when it was first doing the rounds in the clubs all those years ago.

I could feel my old self connecting to my music again – I could sense that familiar thrill. I might have had a fallow period in writing new music, but, by the middle of 2015, TS5 had taken off on a huge scale – it was broadcast on Capital XTRA every Friday, I had toured across Australia with it and, when I brought it live to London, it sold out in less than five minutes.

Doing my TS5 sets to large crowds was nothing short of life-affirming. DJing, mixing other people's records and dropping in my own seemed to set people alive to the beat, and I couldn't get enough of feeling that connection as the crowd danced and partied and, for brief moments, left all their cares behind and gave themselves fully to the whole TS5 experience.

When, in September 2015, I was invited on a BBC Radio 1Xtra session with MistaJam and Kurupt FM, I was pumped and ready to go. As I walked into the studio, Big Narstie was singing to me, '"Booty Man"'s my tune bro! That's my song', referring to the track 'Booty Man' on *Born To Do It*. I loved that he wasn't trying to play it cool, was wearing his heart on his sleeve. And it seemed that the stars aligned as that was the day a freestyle vocal of 'Fill Me In' over the instrumental to Jack Ü's (a partnership between DJs Diplo and Skrillex) 'Where Are Ü Now', featuring Justin Bieber. totally upped the vibe.

There was this spark when I walked into the studio – Stormzy and Shola Ama had just been on – and, for anyone who watched the session, you already know how special it was when the drop hit as I sang the 'Fill Me In' chorus while Big Narstie and the Kurupt guys hyped it on another level from behind me. Wow. There was something beautiful in the air.

By that evening, my performance had gone viral and I was trending on social media (#craigdavidisback), the session getting three-quarters of a million hits overnight. Justin Bieber, Diplo and Skrillex were all tweeting – *Have you seen that performance Craig just did?* Even Scooter Braun, Arianna Grande's manager, got in on the action. Meeting Big Narstie for the first time that day ended up with us getting in the studio and recording 'When the Bassline Drops' a couple of weeks later. I'll never forget the day he came over to the studio to record the song and noticed some of my *Born To Do It* plaques on the floor, leaning up against the wall.

'Craig,' he said, 'why are those plaques all dashed in the corner over there?'

'I just put them there as I was running out of space and didn't wanna be too flash with it all,' I replied.

He then hit me with one of the most profound statements that has lived with me ever since: 'Bro, do you understand what that album meant to me? When I was growing up, that album helped me get through some hard times, helped me to stay out of trouble and inspired me to take this music ting serious! So pick up that plaque and put it up on the wall right now and show it some respect, as that right there [pointing to the plaque] is the reason little black girls and boys all over this country felt seen and inspired to follow their dreams. So, go get a drill and get that up now bro!'

Wow, there wasn't much I could say after that. Blown away by his raw honesty, I went searching for a drill, but even though I couldn't find one in that moment, I've made it my duty to make sure that every plaque I receive now hangs up on the wall in its rightful place, with dignity and honour.

'When the Bassline Drops' went straight into the Top Ten and became Big Narstie's highest chart entry ever. The feeling this gave me was special as Big Narstie's energy that day at 1Xtra really sparked something inside of me. The way he embraced me as soon as I walked in the room, the honesty he shared of how my music was so meaningful to him and the way he schooled me in the studio got me back into my flow. Something had changed, and being back home in the UK and being open to try things differently was working.

After that, I was asked to perform a 'Rewind' medley on the finale show of *The X Factor*. I'll never forget how good that

Something had changed, and being back home in the UK and being open to try things differently was working.

felt – reclaiming that song to an audience of over 8 million, an audience in the UK, many of whom were seeing it for what it was and not how it had been lampooned.

BACK TO BASICS

Now that I was in the UK more than in Miami, I had to decide where to base myself. I wasn't ready to commit to moving back fully and I wasn't ready to pack up my place in the sun, so, as a hybrid, I decided to base myself in the Sofitel. In the end, I was there for more than two years.

This may seem like a strange decision – I had money, I had fame and I had returned to the UK *because* there was an appetite for my music. I was being taken for who I was and what I did, for my inventiveness and the enduring power of my songs. So, why did I stay in a hotel in an airport, when it was no longer necessary for convenience?

The answer, I have come to see now, was that I felt safe there. I had a suite with a bedroom, a sort of living room and a private bathroom. It was warm and cosy and comfortable, and all the facilities I needed – a gym, a restaurant, a spa – were on site. I had access to room service and, every day, my suite was cleaned and gleaming. There was enough room to set up a mini studio – decks and speakers and all the equipment I needed to lay down tracks and vocals. I had my protein shakes, I had my mineral water and I had my favourite white hydrangeas. It was like my room at The Landmark and like my bedroom in Southampton – and the areas I create for myself, wherever they are in the world, however luxurious or basic, and with whatever provisions I have at the time, are my safe spaces. I even loved that it overlooked the hotel car park as this gave me the same feeling I had looking out from my childhood room.

Looking back, what I was doing in the Sofitel was reconnecting with my childhood self. Miami had been a different iteration of 'Me'; I'd arrived bruised, but had repaired myself on the outside – tanned and toned – but, gradually, the veneer began to lose its shine. You can have too much sun, you can mash your body with too many heavy weights and you can only ignore your internal state for so long.

Back in the UK, being contained in the Sofitel, being nearer to my close family and friends, and being back in such close proximity, physically and emotionally, to Colin and his family, made this a very restorative time for me. Back in a room that felt more like home, writing and recording music that made me feel truly alive from deep inside, I was now reconnecting with who I was when I was my best self: my boyhood self, my music-making self, my Notting Hill Carnival self, the self that music flowed effortlessly through and who never questioned himself.

And it worked. I was writing good material and I could feel my creative juices flowing again. I was alive to the pulse that had for so long been quietened and squashed inside me. And that pulse seemed to be beating to the rhythm out there, as, at the beginning of 2016, I signed with Insanity Records, announcing the upcoming release of a new album. I loved being back in the studio and the vibe was everything I could have dreamed of. The result – *Following My Intuition* – became my second Number One album since *Born To Do It* 16 years earlier.

And the music kept coming. When I headlined Glastonbury the following summer, I experienced that same euphoria I had felt at the Notting Hill Carnival. I'd performed there

I was alive to the pulse that had for so long been quietened and squashed inside me.

before, but never on the legendary Pyramid Stage. As I walked out, I saw this sea of faces, arms outstretched, welcoming me, embracing me. I weaved through my band set playing 'Nothing Like This', 'One More Time' and 'When the Bassline Drops' from my new album, even doing a 20-minute TS5 set in between. But something special happened when it came to 'Rewind'. Seeing close to 100,000 people sing it back to me, this crowd – this huge, happy, warm and noisy crowd – here in this moment, going wild for my music – the new and the old – I knew there was no going back. They danced to the rhythm, they sang the lyrics and they lifted me up and carried me to a new place. If you were there that afternoon, thank you. You were there as the light switched on inside me, emotionally.

When I look back at when I moved to Miami to where I ended up in 2015, I can now see the healing process at work: escape, hide, cocoon, restore, realign. I had started the emotional realignment to my music that I'd lost in Miami and had been craving for so long. Being welcomed back, being held by my old audience and now a brand-new generation, my music resonating with them, was something that filled me with the deepest gratitude.

And yet, as I began to connect to my old self, my realignment now an adult version of the creative mind I had been before the darker side of fame made everything wonky, it was all about to come crashing down when my physical self imploded.

SINK OR SWIM

And so we come full circle to me lying in my apartment in Miami in agony, on my back. We flew back there from New York, straight after the slot on *Good Morning America*, a photo shoot and meeting fans in Times Square. I wasn't able to sleep for more than an hour at a time, and sometimes not even an hour through the whole night. Feeling that heavy pain all day and night was as grim as it got. The mix of pills I was taking blocked the pain for a bit here and there, and the stronger ones could even make me forget about it for a few blissful moments, but those times when I had to carry on as normally as I could and that should have been enjoyable, even amazing, were shattered.

A few days later, in Orlando, filming *Ant & Dec's Saturday Night Takeaway*, where I was the DJ for the finale of the UK series, everyone around me hyper and super excited, I spent most of the time in the trailer with Grant finding ways of sitting or lying that didn't make my back spasm. At that point, I was still telling myself that I was meant to be having the time of my life, in this moment, the star guest on Ant and Dec's mega show and I had to 'man up' and 'pull through'. So, I had a word with myself and, despite the nerve endings in my whole body jumping and jangling, firing like sparks from an unearthed plug, I internally grimaced and outwardly smiled through the whole live show.

After Orlando, I made the decision to return to the UK and go back to the Sofitel. After the effort of that journey back home – possibly the most agonising few hours of my life – all I could do was crawl into bed, where I stayed for a few days before embarking on another round of doctors, tests and scans. Again, there was no short-term solution and, after a while, I had to make a choice: stay in my room on my back or try as best as I could to 'get on with it'. I had work to do, a life to lead, people I didn't want to let down. I was still riding high from my comeback, busy promoting my new album *The Time Is Now*, doing interviews and performances, and being visible and present, so I got up and did my positivity thing.

I fooled myself for a couple of days at a time and others for a few more, but I was soon once again back on my back, unable to do anything. Stuck indoors, looking up at the ceiling or the sky with my legs hooked over chairs, trying to get some relief from the pain, wasn't really cutting it.

Being in sharp discomfort 24/7 is physically and mentally exhausting and there was nothing positive about it; the feeling of 240 volts firing off in your back randomly, locking the whole thing up in the process, wears you down. I never knew from one moment to the next which movement was going to cause me unbearable pain. However, what I did know – and what freaked me out to my core – made me panic to the extent that I was nearly out of my mind.

This is what it was. While my recent music comeback had repaired me, given me a reconnection and emotional fulfilment, physically I was now completely marooned. Churning in my mind, maybe for 23 out of 24 hours a day, was that I was slacking. And that slacking was dangerous. That because my mashed-up back meant I couldn't move, I was going to put on weight. That all the training I had done since I'd been terrified of being chubby – at times peaking to the obsessional, but always somewhere close to the edge – would mean my physique would change. I'd lose my six-pack, I'd look out-of-shape, overweight, and then all that reconnection to my music would be for nothing.

Ever since I'd realised that, until I lost weight, I'd be a shoulder to cry on for the girls yearning for the boys with the six-packs; and ever since it had been drummed into me, aged

18, that I needed to be fit and slim and ripped to be worthy of front covers and billboards to maintain my popularity as a singer, I'd stuck to diets and training.

And now, because I couldn't move, I felt that every calorie that was going into my mouth was going into my inert body; that every moment I lay in pain on my back meant my muscle tone was slipping and my body was turning to fat. This was everything I'd worked so hard to swerve, given up so much to achieve, spent so much of my life tuned into. Even the exercises my new trainer, Bevan, was giving me felt lame compared to what I was used to lifting. I'd chosen him to help me get through this because he came with impressive credentials. I'd been told by various doctors that I needed to fire up my paraspinal and multifidus muscles, but this turned out to involve slow, painful exercises that were mindless and repetitive and made me feel useless. I know now that this was me in freefall – Bevan, and my physio Cheyenne, ultimately helped me get through the tedium and I did what I had to do.

I'd always known that the physical is linked to the emotional and now there was no getting around that. Anyone who has been addicted to exercise knows that thrilling endorphin rush that pumps you up during and after a session. If you can't exercise, it affects your mental health. And if part of your mental health is linked to the way you look, then things look pretty bleak. Not only was I suffering a withdrawal of those 'up' hormones, but I also believed that if I didn't get back to my training, the appeal of my music – the part of me I'd only just got back – was going to come to an end. For me, no exercise equalled the end of my career.

I got to a point where I thought that life wasn't worth living, that I would be happier if I wasn't here anymore. There'd be no pain, there'd be no accumulated humiliation, no possibility of *Bo' Selecta!* coming back to take me down again. There'd be no more having to be Mr Positive and Mr Always-Optimistic, vibing so hard it hurt. There'd be no more despair.

But something held me back from the brink. One morning, when the pain had subsided enough for me to get up and face down a day, I realised that I couldn't fix this and I needed help – the kind of help that I'd never asked for before in my entire life. I needed help that wasn't about physio or doctors, people who could fix my back, though I wanted that too. I needed a different sort of help because I could see that this wasn't actually just about my back. It was deeper and broader than that. It was heavier and more burdensome. This was about me at the very core of my being.

With all the hours I had lying on my back, I began to think. I could feel my balance was off because I just wasn't able to be positive. Even when I made myself 'think positively', to try to 'get through' by emitting positive vibes, smiling and straining to greet the pain, telling my friends I was 'fine' and 'would see the pain off', I couldn't do it. And it wasn't working anyway. I

I was in the deep dark blue and I was spiralling.

was in agony and, as the days wore on, my energy levels were depleted. I was in the deep dark blue and I was spiralling.

Sometimes, when you reach a crisis point or something forces you to stop and take a break – from your day-to-day life or from yourself – you begin to see things that you were too busy or too blinkered to see before. You are forced to stare head-on into the darkness. And with all this time on my back and my positive vibes on their knees, I had to recalibrate.

It didn't take me long to put it all together. My positivity was so defensive and sharp and loud, it drowned out any channels to stare down weakness or vulnerability. And even though I'd never spoken this out loud, or whispered it to myself, my fear of negativity was even noisier than my high-octave positivity. But now, laid low and with my back not showing any signs of getting better, I was sapped of any extra energy.

For a few weeks, I kept this all bottled up. I concentrated on the physical – working hard to strengthen my back – but I could hear the stirring, the whispers of the part of me that I thought was impenetrable. My body, the ultra-physical me that I'd worked so hard at and been so committed to for so long – my literal support system – was out the window.

I'd gone for endless MRI scans, PET scans, this treatment, that treatment, one cortisone injection after another to fix my back and I came to realise that I sought quick fixes for all the other downers in my life too. When I wanted a break, I'd fly to the sun. Feeling needy? I'd buy some fresh clothes, have a night out, treat everyone. In the long term they didn't help; they were great distractions and Band-Aid approaches to living, but nothing more.

What I was now understanding was this: if a lot was riding on my back recovering, I knew I had to realign myself in other ways too.

AIN'T GIVING UP

I was at rock bottom and I needed help. I was out of control in the sense that I wasn't able to control what was happening to me both physically and mentally. So I did something I'd never done before – I reached out. I called Colin and told him how desperate I was feeling, and he said: 'Craig, come to my place. I'm here with Amanda and the kids and there's a room for you for as long as you need it. Come and be with us.'

When kindness arrives with that sort of unconditionality, it's like finding an oasis in a desert. You've no idea how I needed to hear those words and how relieved I was that I'd finally admitted out loud that I was in pain beyond the physical. Early in my career when Colin took me on, he promised my nan that he'd always make sure her grandson was looked after. He couldn't, he told her, guarantee that there was going to be success, but he could promise her that there would be protection and care. And he was true to his word from day one – he'd always been there for me, welcoming me into his family, and we had a great, easy, comfortable relationship. But – and this was *my* weakness, my inability or unwillingness to face down the negative – I'd always made sure that I was undemanding in an emotional sense, always positive and up for whatever was going on.

So showing him my vulnerability was the first step for me. The conversations we had from that moment of me asking for help weren't about music or business. They were about me, scooped-up, hollowed-out, looking down at the ground and, eventually, into his eyes, telling him that I'd never felt this kind of pain before and I'd never been head-on in a situation where the word depression kept coming into my head.

In a period of pivotal moments, this was probably the most pivotal of them all. To break through the need to be in control, to allow myself a deeper relationship with Colin who was so present, so *there* for me, was a revelation, and I hadn't really understood before how that played out. This was a real moment of breaking through the façade that I'd created and the lifelong fortress I'd erected against being vulnerable or overtly emotional. Right from the moment I'd met Colin, he'd been like a father to me. And I'd been like his son, only a son who had wanted to dazzle and please, striving for praise, never showing my true feelings. I know now that Colin saw through that and was so skilled in reading me that he guided me while never letting me see he was acknowledging my vulnerability.

Without a solution for the pain, I felt out of control. But being able to talk to Colin, to see Colin holding my space, I began to feel as though I could find a way back up from the pit of despair, from my dark night of the soul. It was as if by opening this dialogue – out loud and inside my mind – I suddenly had permission – from myself, and now from others around me – to let go and explore the possibility of relinquishing that iron grip I'd had on being positive. I guess it was helped by the fact that the physical pain was still draining so much energy from me that, in truth, even I would have found it hard to put a positive spin on it.

One of the first things Colin told me to do was to stop hiding in the Sofitel – to find a home, a place that was filled with light, a place I could make my own. He and Amanda set about helping me look and, while it took a while for me to find the right one (yes, I am a bit of an obsessive perfectionist when it comes to interiors), I eventually found the place I'm in now. I bought it in 2019 and moved in during that year. Finding a place to put down new roots was important and I couldn't be more grateful that Colin steered me to a sanctuary and safe space of my own.

It's funny because the pain I was experiencing – the actuality of it and the moving carefully to try not to trigger it – heightened my sense of what my body was going through and tuned me into listening to it more carefully. And even though what I was hearing was discordant, the process of slowing down and leaning in brought me back into my body.

Back in Miami when Jill opened my eyes to the inspirational words of Brené Brown, while at first I had been sceptical – *why would I want to lean into any sort of vulnerability when I prided myself on doing all I could to make myself seem positive and strong, impenetrable even?* – I had, at least, listened to what she had to say. As I leaned into these new ideas, I realised that it's good to shake things up and that opening myself up to other ways of thinking and coming out of my filter bubble was a positive thing.

Now, at a time when I needed wisdom more than ever, I was experiencing a deeper, spiritual aspect that was beginning to give me some answers that the physical couldn't. Through my reading and exploration, I discovered how and in what circumstances this dark night of the soul happened to other people; that they, too, had gone through moments when their whole world was spun upside down and, in different ways, they had also been forced to relinquish control. And by doing so, each of them had spiralled down into dark places, but something – some force, some sort of spiritual or emotional revelation – had occurred and they'd come back.

Even just opening myself up to the minds and spirits of these teachers was a revelation – something I would recommend to you if you're going through any sort of change or situation in which you need some fresh perspective. Some of these books are beautiful, flowing reads – and a lot of what I took in came through audiobooks, TV programmes, podcasts and online talks. And, sometimes, new perspectives came from surprising places.

TEARDROPS

It was while watching a Pixar movie – *Inside Out* – that I had an epiphany. For me, this movie contains multitudes. If you've seen it, you'll feel my vibe on this; and if you haven't, you *must*. It's about an 11-year-old girl who has to move from one town to another because of her father's job, and her reluctance and sadness at having to do so. The movie is set inside her brain, as all five of her main emotions – Anger, Disgust, Fear, Sadness and Joy – jostle with each other as she comes to make sense of, and experience, the big move.

The genius of the storyline – and the genius of *Pixar* that children and adults can relate to their movies on different levels – is that it makes it crystal clear that we need all of our emotions, not just the positive ones, to navigate through life. That all of our emotions serve a purpose and, if we refuse to face our negative thoughts or keep swerving them by straining to be positive all the time, we will get stuck in certain places. And that, ultimately, while we have little control over our emotions, we *can* choose what we do about them.

Maybe at certain times in our lives, it takes an animated, brightly-coloured, brilliantly voiced, visual representation of our feelings and emotions to strike a chord and bring home what has been bothering us; to realise that, despite our age and experience and so-called wisdom or insight, it can still be hard to make good decisions because our feelings are so powerful and there are so many fighting to be heard. For me, that centred around my electrifying fear of being negative, of not *always* exuding positivity.

You know the feeling – telling yourself you have to be Mr/ Ms Positive in this thing, but your circumstances are telling you this really isn't positive and there's nothing you can do to reframe it to make it instantly right.

I'd lived all my life to that point drowning out any emotion that wasn't upbeat. I was all about the Outside Out, squashing down my Inside In, but lying on my back with plenty of time to ruminate, I was forced to come to terms with the way I dealt with my emotions, especially the positive and the negative.

I see it like a magnet – if you take a long magnet and you start shaving parts off, however small it gets, it's still going to have positive and negative polarities. The more you deny that one part doesn't exist – in my case, negativity – the more you're just playing yourself and, up to *Good Morning America*, I played myself thinking there was no such thing as negativity. I was so intent on finding the positive in everything that, in the end – and the end was now – it was unsustainable.

As soon as it hit me that the magnet will always contain the positive *and* the negative, I realised that accepting negativity for a negative situation was actually accepting the real understanding of being positive. It was weird and back to front; a paradox of what I'd always thought positivity was. I had to now accept that when I walked onto that stage and all that followed, that I'd felt something I'd never felt before and that there was no way of reframing it to feel positive. I had to lean into that feeling of pain and the wash of negativity that came with it.

Maybe you recognise this – that with all the messages out there to 'be positive', to 'embrace your positivity', you too are, or have been, afraid of confronting the negative. But there are times when you don't need to be positive, when you don't need to push through to be positive, that it is actually better to accept that the situation you're in right now isn't that great, that it is what it is. In fact, too much positivity can be a negative thing. Reframing your outlook comes from accepting both the positive *and* the negative. That acceptance will allow you to treat yourself with greater care. With easing back, all the anxiety that comes when you're straining to be positive will dissolve.

It's amazing when you finally realise something about yourself and start – however slowly and, trust me, I was taking snail steps – to think about it and let it settle and mull around in your mind. It's refreshing and rewarding to accept what's going on and see it for what it is.

Trust me. It's in adversity that you find your true character and, when I look back to my back-'breaking' *Good Morning America* moment, I'm like, *Wow – you had so much to learn. You really did think you knew yourself, but you didn't.* And I realise how fortunate I was to have experienced that and, if I hadn't, I'd still be living that high-tension life of never being able to be anything other than shiny-bright and positive; way off-kilter, off balance and never true to who I didn't then know myself to be.

This was my window on to the rest of my life. And if this hadn't happened, who knows where I'd be today.

Reframing your outlook comes from accepting both the positive *and* the negative.

CHAPTER NINE
Following My Intuition

It was a combination of having spent this period listening to my body, being more in tune with my inner self, my epiphanic realisation that I could dial down my relentless external positivity and the resonance of having always somewhere leaned into my vibes, that delivered me to the spiritual teacher and visionary guide, Sonia Choquette.

Of all the inspirational teachers who I read or listened to, it was Sonia's teachings that spoke most to me, stirring something deep inside and making me want to find out more. I needed wisdom and insight that was practical as well as spiritual. I read and reread her brilliant book *Trust Your Vibes*, listened to her talks online and then, because I wanted to know more, I reached out and booked a phone session with her.

As soon as I heard Sonia's voice I felt comfortable and, when we began to talk, it was like this light went on inside me. I loved the way she described how she was encouraged to tap into her sixth sense from a very early age and to trust her intuition above everything else. When she was a little girl, she told me, at supper each evening, the first question her mother would ask her and her seven siblings was how their vibes had been that day. Not, 'How did you do in your maths test?' Or, 'Who did you play with?' But, 'How were your vibes today? What did you pick up? What resonated with you?' This all struck a chord with me as I also use this type of language whenever I walk into a recording session and ask everyone in the room, 'What's your vibe?' Sonia then told me how remarkable her mother was and how much she admired her. A child refugee, she'd survived the harsh conditions of World War Two, got married at 15 and lost her hearing during her journey from Romania to America. In order to survive, she told her children, she'd had to rely on her intuition and it had never let her down. Helping them tap into theirs and be guided by it was the single most precious gift she believed she could pass on to them.

When Sonia gently asked if I'd thought about the possibility of opening up and accessing my intuition, 'this sixth sense we all have but don't all know how to tap into', I was ready to listen. This idea of tapping into my inner energy resonated. It was as if I was hearing what had been rumbling somewhere inside me, but I'd never been able to articulate or tune into it in the way I'd like. It had always come in glimpses, like back when I was about 12, I found myself walking a certain way out of my estate to the park, convinced that I was going to find some money in one particular spot. For weeks, despite my eyes being out on stalks, looking so hard and feeling this bitter disappointment when nothing materialised, sometime later, when I was still walking that way but had kind of lost heart, I noticed something on the ground. It was a £20 note. I couldn't believe it, but, at the same time, it was like, 'Oh, hello £20 note, I knew I'd run into you here at some point.' There was something in my gut that made me always go that way, look in that specific spot, tune in and, without any conscious reasoning, follow my instinct.

Equally, there had been times in my life when I wished I'd followed my gut feeling. There were times when, even years later, I was still kicking myself for not listening to what my intuition was telling me, but instead was frozen by what my brain dictated – what I thought made the most sense at the time, even if it felt wrong. One such moment even inspired me to write a song, 20 years later.

Picture the scene. Me in my navy blue school uniform, 15 years old and running as fast as I could to get the number 5 bus, just as it pulled away from the bus stop with all my mates on it. Fresh out of breath, I thought about hurtling as fast as I could to the next stop when I caught sight of a girl about the same age as me waiting at the stop opposite. She was looking right at me. In less than a second, my decision was made. I just knew I had to stay right where I was and wait for the next bus. The vibes were so instant, I could almost see them sparking across the busy road, past bikes, over cars, under lorries. I looked at her, she looked at me, I looked away; I looked back at her, she looked away; I looked down, she looked up ... You know what I'm talking about. There was something so radiant about her and there were butterflies in my tummy. I was hot and cold and that beautiful moment of infinite possibility stretched out in front of me.

The number 5 wasn't that reliable, so I knew I had a bit of time. I also knew I was going to be late for registration, but that didn't matter. No. My inner voice was telling me to go over and swap numbers with her before her bus came. But as I tried to put one foot in front of the other, I kind of felt myself stutter, my movements clumsy, awkward. As I looked over, she was smiling, an open invitation of *When are you going to come over and say hi?* But I was frozen. Even as I had an internal word with myself along the lines of: *You idiot, go over and say hi; what's the matter with you?*, a more insistent voice was telling me, *Nah, she won't call, she won't want your number, she's just messing with you.*

And then her bus came – out of nowhere, but it was there. And just before it obscured her from my view, she gave me this look of regret, like, *I've read this wrong, maybe you aren't interested in me after all.* She got on the bus, and I watched her walk down the aisle and take a seat by the window. As the bus pulled away, she looked at me and in her face were a thousand looks of 'what if?', and that's when I started kicking myself. Why hadn't I just listened to what my heart was telling me?

We've all been there, right? That disappointment I felt after, of asking myself over and over again for days, weeks, *years*, yesterday, why I hadn't hopped over the road to get her number, was formative and, in hindsight, taught me a lot. I've come to see that, even if I'd gone over and had read the vibes wrong and she'd told me where to go, I would have at least felt that uplift I now know you get when you listen to what your heart and soul are telling you. No regrets, no wondering, 'what if?'

I still think about that bus stop moment and somewhere, deep down, I'm still kicking myself that I didn't cross the street and say hi to her. It's not that I think the course of my life would have changed or that I'm such a romantic to think that today we'd be married with a couple of kids. But it was such a memorable moment and I can still see and feel it so sharply down the years, and the agony of me being too closed up and unaware that I could listen to my intuition haunts me. At least I got a song out of it.

'What If' was my tribute to that girl waiting for her bus and to that moment when I didn't listen to my inner voice.

It's amazing isn't it, in our action-packed lives, how some moments stick out more than others and stay with us? Maybe even, in time, they act as catalysts for us to change and learn and grow from, even if it's years later.

Trust me, it took a long, long time from the number 5 bus stop in Southampton to writing that song before I was ready to fully acknowledge, tap into and then begin to act on my intuition. And I'm very glad that I have.

ALREADY KNOW

Intuition is a powerful thing and it's so much a part of who I am now. Following my heart has allowed me to release the control I was allowing my rational thoughts to have on all aspects of my life. Take my latest album, *22*. While I was mixing one of my tracks from it – 'My Heart's Been Waiting

Intuition is a powerful thing and it's so much a part of who I am now.

For You' – I got sent a remix by a producer called Duvall. Four things happened: I listened to it, I loved the vibe, I saw the word 'Disciples' (Duvall's group) and, on top of that, he had titled his email 'Feel that love', a lyric from the song. Usually, I would have put this one in the remix pile and done my usual thing of listening to all the options that were coming in. But I knew there and then that this was the version I was going to record. I got the signs and I honoured them.

We all have a lower self and a higher self. If that sounds wafty or a bit 'woo-woo', stay with me and maybe, like me, imagine it visually. For me, it's as if my lower self is the bass notes of the piano and my higher self is all the way up the keyboard – those beautiful high notes. The thing is that we all have a higher octave version of ourselves, which is our intuition – that wiser part of us that always has our back and can see so much more of the bigger picture, telling us to go say hi, cross the road, don't stand on the other side like a joker – but the only way we can hear it is when the lower notes – the part of us that loves to overthink, doubt and worry – are quietened.

We are all spiritual beings and we all have this sixth sense along with our five other senses, and we need this sixth sense – our high vibes – to be active, so we can be fulfilled, happy and peaceful. All we need to do to turn it on and turn it up, is to tune in and activate it, and then use it, just like we use our other senses. It's a bit like taking advantage of an inner Waze or GPS – that extra help to navigate where we need to be.

Intuition is as real as touch, taste, smell, sight and hearing, and, because it is a part of us, I'm passionate about using this incredible innate tool that is spiritual, centred in our heart, connecting our soul to the beautiful spiritual forces that are guiding us through life.

Have you ever felt that you're an old soul or someone has told you so? We tend to interpret that as meaning that we have learned a few lessons early or have acquired some sort of wisdom that seems beyond our years. Well, there's some truth in that – learning and experiencing things definitely give us the ability to look at similar situations with a sense of hindsight. But what if it was more than this? What if this wasn't our first rendezvous (no pun intended) here on earth? This would also answer why we can have such beautiful, rich soul connections – that somehow transcend time – with people who we may have only just met, which can feel deeper than with a family member we've known all our lives. This is because we have a soul family – a group of souls that jump back in with us time after time and help each other at various stages. I spoke about this with Regina Meredith, a metaphysical interviewer and intuitive, on her podcast. It was beautiful to dive into subjects like reincarnation, soul mates and soul agreements and not see that blank look that I've experienced so many times when you know the other person isn't really ready to go there or genuinely has no interest in what you're going on about. But that's OK as some things aren't for everyone and should come at the right divine time, but when you have the chance to really deep-dive with someone who shares your common interest, I suggest doing it as much as you can as it makes life seem more vivid, magical and colourful.

When you access your more spiritual side like this, then, trust me, you start to move differently. You start to get a real sense of communion with yourself, with life; you start to sense the way that your energy flows, how the currents of the inner-you stream. Maybe you know that feeling – a place or situation you're sometimes in, where things just make sense, they just flow. It happens for me in the studio when I'm writing music and I'm fully in the moment; I'm not thinking, I'm not even hearing. It's a *knowing*. I just know I have to get to that note, I just know when I've hit the right melody and, as soon as I do, it feels like I've got the memo and something inside of me lights up.

This isn't an inner arrogance telling me that I'm right about everything (because I am not). This isn't about a supreme confidence that my inner voice bestows on me to do the right thing in that moment for myself. This is different. This is me tapping into my inner voice, trusting my spiritual and inner energy. It's me using my heart intelligence – my spirit – feeling the greater pull of the universe. Don't worry, I'm not using the word 'spirit' in a scary way. For me, spirit is the breath we take, the essence that gives each of us our existence and helps guide us through life making the right decisions for ourselves.

Like me, you might find that, at first, your intuition seems more difficult to tap into than, say, a lovely meal that excites our taste buds or a beautiful song that is music to our ears, because our ego loves to get in the way of unfamiliar senses. It's a bit like an overprotective parent trying to keep everything safe and under control. Our ego isn't a bad thing – it serves a purpose – but just as a puppy doesn't know any better, when it comes to why it's barking, our ego has to be trained to understand that it can relax and know that it's being looked after.

There have been several times in the past when I've wanted to try something new, but, as soon as I took that first step forward, this loud warning voice went off on one, to the point where my next step ended up going backwards: *Don't go there, it's dangerous; don't try that, remember what happened before.* I guess that's why I wrote the song '2 Steps Back' on my album *Slicker than Your Average* back in 2002, as, even then, I could intuitively feel the difference between my ego and my sixth sense. One always felt super loud in trying to protect me, while the other was much quieter, yet somehow more confident, sure and consistent in its guidance, like it already knew what was on the other side of all the don'ts.

Leaning into my intuition has definitely been more of an adventure – playful and fun – and I know it will be the same for you too. Because I know, when my intuition takes one step forward, it's only my ego that wants to take two steps back. And every time my intuition is right. Trust me.

So, how do we quieten our egos? How, for example, do we block out the sound of our minds telling us we aren't good enough, clever enough, good-looking enough, fit enough ... the list goes on? How do we quieten the negative self-talk and that imposter syndrome many of us feel? The answer, I have found, is straightforward: we have to learn to be present enough to listen to our intuition and what it's telling us and trust where it might lead if we act on what we hear.

One way to do this is by stilling our minds, so that we bring ourselves into the present, so the barking puppy can chill out and get some rest. By taking a deep breath in and a deep breath out, and then looking around us for something new to notice, we immediately stop thinking and instead start to feel aware, present and calmer. This allows us some space to tune into our inner voice and lean into our intuition. I'm in my studio and I'm doing it now and I can see the weaving in my microphone, something I've not noticed before, even though I spend so much time with it right in front of my face. Looking at it like this, I can sense my inner vibes shifting.

Try it. Stop reading, breathe in and breathe out, then fix your stare on something in your room. A photo frame, for example. Yes, you know what's inside the frame; you might have looked at that photo every day since you took it and framed it. But have you ever looked at the shine or the silver or the pattern of the frame that houses it? Stay there for a few moments and take it all in. Now, look away, breathe in and breathe out and see how you feel.

What did you notice? What did you see that you have missed before? I wish I could hear what you are telling yourself, that I was there experiencing this moment of seeing with you.

I love it. I love the feeling of quiet and also inner excitement it brings me, like I'm seeing something small and exquisite, even if that's the knit of the material around my microphone. And because I've been doing this for a while now, I know that if I carry on looking, I'll pick up even smaller intricacies and, believe me, no detail can be too small to appreciate, even for just a few seconds.

Now you are in the moment, from this place you can really tap into your intuition. Maybe something has come up for you, beyond the detail of the frame; maybe a thought, a feeling, a sound has emerged from inside you. Whatever it is, you are in the right place to receive that gut feeling. What is it telling you? What feels right?

The magic of quietening your ego and blocking out external thoughts to hear your inner voice can't be underestimated. And I get that, after a while, my microphone may not be the most interesting thing in the world, but I have found that this technique is a good stepping stone to slowing myself down, not being in a rush and having the time and space to listen to what my heart is telling me. And this allows me to begin that tap-tapping into my intuition.

LAST NIGHT

What I found most helpful when I started to listen in on what my intuition was telling me was to journal my thoughts and dreams. I was a bit of a slow starter on this, but, once you commit, it's super easy to incorporate into your everyday routine and becomes habit in less than a couple of weeks. Journaling has become such a key part of my life now.

The key to harnessing your inner voice and tapping into it so it becomes your accessible sixth sense is to chart your thoughts and dreams, however random, and to have the courage – and the discipline – to start this off.

You can use a notebook or an electronic device to journal your thoughts and dreams or, to make it even easier, you can leave yourself a voice note as these only a take a moment and you can always listen back. For me, I've found that having what I call my 'vibes notebooks' – and I choose them specifically for this – can sometimes be better than using my phone or computer. There's something more connecting about writing my thoughts with a pen onto paper; it gives credible evidence to the repeating themes I see or gives voice to something that resonates when I come back for validation.

When I was a kid, I loved Southampton F.C. – I still do. As well as our fish-and-chips-Blockbuster Friday nights, when we could afford it, my mum and I would go to The Dell to watch them play. Like collecting stamps and making lists of where records were in the charts, I loved getting autographs and, after the matches, my mum and I would wait for players to come out so I could present them with my little book and the pen I always remembered to bring with me. I was nothing if not persistent and, while it took several goes and hours' worth of queuing post-match, I managed to get Alan Shearer's – the Saints' star striker (this was back in the day) – autograph and, a couple of times, some of the visiting players', including Gary Lineker's when he played for Tottenham, and Jamie Redknapp's, when he was at Liverpool.

But more than this, I would dream hours away, imagining me scoring goals for the Saints, my name a local legend for my skills on the pitch. I was a good footballer and played for my school team, and while I was realistic enough to know I was never going to be a *great* footballer, I still had that innocent optimism to be able to dream the dream.

Whenever I had to draw in class, I drew myself on the pitch, wearing the red and white of my team; whenever I had to say what I wanted to be when I grew up, I'd say a DJ *and* a footballer, youthfully figuring I could play in the day and DJ at night – and I wrote lyrics about being the goal-scoring hero at The Dell. I wrote stories about playing for the Saints, I would walk around thinking about tactics and I had this recurring dream that I was called and asked to play for the team. This dream was so vivid that I actually felt the shirt against my skin, the pass of the ball; I could hear the encouragement of my

The key to harnessing your inner voice is to chart your thoughts and dreams.

heroes, now my teammates, and the noise of the crowd as they cheered us on. The repetitive thread of this dream was that I was always running late, trying to get on my shin pads and boots as the starting whistle sounded. I'd have to dash onto the pitch, startled and unready. Once on, though, I shimmied and nutmegged my way to goal-scoring glory – the hero of the game. The beauty of dreamland is that not all parts make sense, but you go with it. All I knew was that, when I woke up, I was, for a few moments, completely content, lying still, while I played the action back in my mind.

Fast forward to 2008, and how could I have imagined that I would play for Soccer Aid at Wembley with my England shirt on (I'd never even dared dream of playing for my country)? I was on the bench for the first part of the match, caught up in the excitement on the pitch, when I was told I was going on. So there I was, trying to get on my shin pads and boots in gestures that were an echo from my childhood dream, and as

I ran onto the pitch to the cheer of the crowd, imagine what was going on inside me as my first touch of the ball came from a pass from Jamie Redknapp, and my first pass sent the ball to Alan Shearer. And when I was one-on-one with the goalkeeper, the crowd of 60,000 cheering me on to score, in that moment when I lifted my leg and struck the ball, the goalkeeper off his line, it was happening – I was in my dream. 'It's going in,' I said to myself. But the ball continued to rise and rise, with no sign of falling, until it cleared the crossbar and ended its magnificent journey way up in the top tier of the stand. Not quite how I had seen it in my dream. However, when, at the end of the game, I was named Man of the Match, I had to stop myself from telling the whole of Wembley how my dream had manifested itself.

Charting your dreams is solid, trust me. Say you wake up one morning and you've had this vivid dream and it's still with you as you get up, before you do anything else, reach for your notebook by the side of your bed and write it down. I'm not saying that you have to write it out in full like an essay or you have to go into some deep creative writing. No overthinking or hard work is required. It's all about chronicling – in words, short phrases or even in drawings – what your mind and heart are telling you; to give it form, to notice it.

You can do this with your thoughts too. If thoughts come up in the day – while you're out on a walk or fixing something or cooking – and you feel you want to reach for your phone and record them (or, if you have time, write them down), do it. And in that charting, you might then notice patterns, other messages or thoughts that come in and around them; other conversations or incoming thoughts in the day or days that follow that chime or resonate with what you've written down. And that's how your inner voice speaks, through repetition of messages, someone saying the same thing that you hear in different iterations. It actually makes life so magical and exciting. The hardest thing is that, if you aren't using certain practices to ground yourself, to be present, to hear your inner voice, you'll miss it.

Say you have a new idea – maybe that you want to start something new: a new job, business or relationship; or make some changes in your life; or move to a new place, as I did when I made the move back from Miami to the UK; or retrain to do something different – unless it's straightforward, there'll be all sorts of doubts that start clamouring for attention in your head: *it's too risky; it's too far; there's too much at stake; I'm too old/too young; they won't want to come with me* … You know what I'm talking about. The rational, loud side of you will be like that barking dog, and that's all you will be able to hear.

If that happens now, I try to quieten that noise. I'm not saying it's wrong – that place on the other side of town might not be right for all sorts of reasons – but, before I give into it (and it's always too loud), I try to still it, to calm it down, so

I can tune into my inner vibe. And I've found that in writing down my dreams and thoughts, when I've been contemplating big or even small changes or decisions, before I make up my mind, I look through and see if anything chimes, whether my heart and soul are telling me something different to what my logical brain is dictating.

And you know what? Often, there's something there.

For a time I was feeling tired a lot. Weeks before seeing the doctor, I must have seen four buses in one day with the same advertisement for iron pills displayed on the back. The next day, while watching YouTube, the advert between the music videos was trying to sell some sort of new steam iron for clothes. Later that day, a mate came over and wanted to watch a movie. What did he want to watch? *Iron Man 2*.

I'd written these things down and it was only when I was going back over some recent entries that it hit me. I knew what I needed to do. And so I went to see my doctor and, after taking my bloods, it was no surprise when he prescribed iron supplements. This is how it works. These messages come through all the time and, when we write them down and see the themes and repetitions in front of us, we can make sense of these signs and guidance.

I also write down my thoughts after swimming or coming back from a long walk, as that's when they come into my mind. Any time your mind is stilled, listen in and see what your heart and soul are telling you. It's amazing what's in there.

MAGIC

Learning to listen in and hear my inner voice is one of the most rewarding things I've ever done. I'm still a journeyman on this road, still learning to listen into my inner sense and how to put it into practice more completely.

Believe me, if I can do it, so can you. It's all about being willing and open and leaning in, practising the techniques I've walked us through and being tuned into times when you can act on what your intuition is telling you. Sometimes, when you do, the outcome can be beautiful – both for you and for those around you.

Take something that happened during the first coronavirus lockdown in April 2020. I live on a small street and, because we were all finding it so new and strange, I wanted

I'm still learning to listen into my inner sense and how to put it into practice more completely.

to reach out to my neighbours and make sure that those who were vulnerable were being taken care of. My housekeeper Gina – who, I am happy to say, had come back as soon as I moved into my new home – is brilliant at making connections and, because she knows my vibe, is always on hand to help me send little gifts and good vibe messages to my neighbours. So I wrote some notes and Gina posted them through the neighbours' letterboxes. It turned out that three of the people living close to us did need some help. We shopped and cooked for them and, when we took over our care packages and stood behind our masks, socially distanced from their front doors, we struck up conversations, and soon friendships were made. You may have experienced this vibe yourself in the early days of lockdown when neighbours came together and helped each other out. I've got to say that this was one aspect of lockdown that bound us together more and, for some of us, continues to this day.

One of our neighbours, a lovely Portuguese lady in her late seventies, who was always so pleased to see us, had told us on our first visit to her front door that her daughter had died of cancer a couple of weeks before lockdown started and, because of the restrictions, she hadn't been able to fly back to Portugal for the funeral. More heartbreakingly, she hadn't been able to be by her daughter's bedside in the last days of her life. She was so dignified in her grief, never wanting to burden us, and as we couldn't go in and sit down with her, we took particular care to watch out for her and deliver a few extra goodies.

One morning, a few weeks after we'd met, I had this feeling that I needed to give her something that was a bit more personal. I was cleaning my teeth and all I could hear was my inner voice telling me, gently and insistently, 'Portugal, Portugal'. Right, I thought, let me look at some pictures of Portugal. Wow. I was overwhelmed by beautiful images – sandy coves and beaches, deep blue sea, colourful fishing villages, seaside resorts, cathedrals in old towns and delicious-looking food.

There was one photo that stood out and I knew that this was the one I wanted to buy, download and frame for her. It was of São Vicente, a mountain village on Madeira, and I had the perfect frame for it. I then had this overwhelming desire to write a note to her with the words, 'Keep letting the world see that beautiful smile of yours Hilda'. Or, I paused, was it 'Ilda'?

Something was pushing me to check that I was spelling her name correctly – was it with an 'H' or an 'I'? – so I asked Gina to check by looking through their WhatsApp chats. None seemed to be signed off with her name and yet it was clear to me that I had to make sure it was right. I even thought of leaving her name off as it would have been easier, but that wasn't the vibe. So Gina offered to go across the road to ask one of our neighbours. She returned adamant that it was 'Hilda' with an 'H'. So, I went back upstairs, printed and perfected the image and put it in the frame.

But it still didn't feel quite right. After an hour of sitting with it, I remembered a note that Hilda – or was it Ilda? – had given me when I'd moved in, but I had no idea where it was. Then again, I got this urge to look in a drawer in my studio, a drawer containing fragments of lyrics, studio equipment manuals and other paraphernalia. And there was the note: 'Ilda' … with an 'I'. It seemed like the whole street needed a new memo.

Now that the photo was framed, the frame wrapped and the note written with the correct spelling of Ilda's name, I asked Gina to take it across to her as I didn't want to interfere in the moment she opened it – her having to give her energy to being thankful; I just wanted her to be present in herself as she unwrapped it. So Gina went over, knocked on the door, set the gift down and backed away. As she turned to come back, Ilda came out and, as she always did, greeted Gina with a big smile. But instead of going back inside like she usually did, Ilda opened the gift. She looked at the picture and tears began to roll down her cheeks.

'Gina,' she said, 'today was Maggie's birthday. And this,' she gestured to the picture, 'was where we used to go on holiday together. How did you *know*? How did you *know* that today I woke up and thought about this place and the two of us there together and now here is this picture and I can feel my daughter with me? How did you *know* that today of all days was the day I needed this encouragement to "keep smiling", that my daughter always called my smile beautiful? How did Craig *know* this?'

I didn't know. I didn't know the facts – that this was her daughter's birthday or that São Vicente was the place they went to together. But I'd woken up that morning and what I did know was that my intuition was telling me that today Ilda needed me to reach out to her. I trusted my intuition and it came good for her and, if you believe as I do (and I appreciate that for some of you this will be a stretch), that, in all of this, Ilda's daughter was reaching out to her mum, then you will understand just how beautiful that morning was.

Moments like this have shown me how the sum of our intuitive parts makes our lives take on a much deeper meaning. It's like having a friend, always there to help us, regardless of the situation. When we know how to trust our intuition and, more importantly, to act on it, every day has the potential to become more magical – for ourselves and for others.

And to the girl – frozen in time and memory – at the number 5 bus stop, if you're reading this, thank you for being there that day. You've been an inspiration.

CHAPTER TEN

Somebody Like Me

On my 39th birthday, which also fell in those first lockdown days, I joined a Zoom meeting. As I logged on and saw a whole load of friends and colleagues from our management team, recording studio and my band, it became apparent that a surprise virtual gathering had been arranged for me. A cake appeared behind me from Gina who was in on the whole surprise and I felt this warm glow of gratitude that they'd all showed up. After a bit of Zoom awkwardness, Kwame – the musical director of my band – struck a chord on his guitar. They all burst into 'Happy Birthday' and, even with all that distorted out-of-sync virtual singing, it was beautiful to hear their voices and watch their faces.

As they finished, there was this sort of silence. No one spoke. You know that Zoom thing – we all went through it in one way or another as we struggled to make things work over that period. But, for some reason, rather than kicking back and enjoying being serenaded to, I instead felt this compulsive urge to fill the awkward silence. 'Play another chord, my man,' I said to Kwame. And just as if I was transitioning from a song on stage, the autopilot in me went into full performance mode.

For the next eternity, as everyone sat there, patience frozen onto their faces, I sung an ad-libbed, made-up, on-the-spot thank you to each and every one of them. And as I got further and deeper into it, I had to become more inventive with the melodies and lyrics.

As I travelled around the screen, I could see a degree of pleasure in everyone's faces as they were having their own personal thank you delivered to them. But something in me was also aware of the other 15 faces still to go and I was wondering why the hell I had started this. I knew I wasn't going to stop until I had sung to them all, but I had this uncomfortable feeling that all they wanted to do was get off the call and be anywhere other than trapped in a little box-frame on my computer watching me go through this. I could see how exhausted Kwame was, having to hang around while I freestyled my way through everyone and no doubt a bit of him and everyone else died inside as they realised how long they'd have to wait.

Eventually – and it felt like a couple of birthdays had passed – I finished. There was this look of release on every-one's faces. I gazed into the screen and smiled, just as I should have at the start, and, unsurprisingly, the call came to its natural end. 'Happy Birthday Craig ...', everyone shouted, 'have a great day!'

I sat there on my couch, trying to process how this beautiful gesture from my friends had turned into a full-on performance from me. What had just happened? Now a sweaty mess, I looked at the time and realised that there were only a couple of hours until I had to do a live TS5 set on Instagram and Facebook Live – a nice little idea that I felt would be fun for my fans and a way to make my birthday a little more exciting than being locked down at home alone, in my sweat pants, watching a movie, with a cake-for-one in front of me.

With the time ticking down and having already announced on social media earlier in the day that I was going to be doing something special, any ideas for a birthday swim, walk, chill and relax were gone. So I hotfooted it up to my home studio and ran through the set, got myself looking reasonable and, with about half an hour to go, dialled up my tech guys. Going up on Instagram and Facebook Live wasn't as straightforward as I'd imagined, they explained, especially as I wanted the sound to be pristine – I mean, why make things easy for myself, especially on my birthday? *Oh no, we can't just do the show using my regular phone camera and microphone; no, no, we've got to go through my whole studio set-up to make it sound amazing.* I ended up downloading some wonky app that promised to make all this work seamlessly.

With 20 minutes to go, I was feeling slightly calmer. I did the final checks – sound, good; visuals, looking great. The last thing was to get logged in and I was good to go. Or so I thought. 'Um, Craig,' came a message from the tech team. 'We can't access your Instagram or FB as it keeps logging us out.'

Ten minutes to go, five minutes, and I was standing there in my studio, sweating for England with nothing going to plan. The professional in me is a perfectionist and there was no way I was going to let anyone down, so I had to think on my feet. I decided that, while the tech guys were trying to get things to work, I'd jump straight on my Insta, old-school style, and warm everyone up – my mic in one hand while trying to play some instrumentals out of my speakers and vibe over them until both streams were ready. After 20 minutes of trying to DJ and sing while simultaneously looking at my computer screen to see if the tech guys were having any luck, I felt the pressure mounting.

Part of me was thinking: *This has gone completely pear-shaped and I might as well just turn this all off and call it a day.* But, strangely enough, out of my comfort zone, I felt a kind of high from the challenge setting in. So I kept going.

After half an hour, the tech team could access my Facebook. But then came the message: 'Insta ... still logging us out.'

So, here I was performing into my phone camera for Insta while simultaneously performing into my computer screen with my studio mic for Facebook. I mean talk about being completely frazzled for the next hour and a half.

The two things that kept me going were the adrenaline coursing through my body and the positive energy from all the fans who tuned in. It turned out to be a great set and I was hyped by the vibes coming in as I performed – the happy birthday love, the 'we're-loving-this' messages and the whole buzz. I finished on a high.

But later, lying on the sofa in my studio, I felt broken, sapped of all energy, unable even to read messages from my friends and family or open any presents they'd sent. Queuing at a post office required a mammoth effort in those lockdown days and some friends had even walked over and left things on the doorstep for me. But all those sentiments lay unwrapped on the kitchen table and I was too tired to go downstairs to get them. I'd spent all day singing to everyone as if it was *their* birthday and now all I wanted to do was crawl into bed and shut down the day.

It was later the next morning when I was swimming that I reflected back on what had happened. Why, when it had started out so beautifully – a surprise cake, Colin inviting me on to the Zoom, a short set in the evening, calm – did it feel like it had all gone so wonky that I'd ended up wishing the day had never begun?

HIDDEN AGENDA

For many years – through good times and bad; record sales ups and downs – I have said yes when I meant no, I have put the needs of others before my own, I've worn myself out pleasing them. And while, as you will see, I've begun to address this and change my behaviour to make life easier for myself and others around me, old habits die hard and, on my birthday, I regressed.

This much I knew: it needn't have turned out like that. All I'd had to do was show up on the Zoom call, receive the heartfelt sentiment of my friends' happy birthday vibes, say thank you and go. Any brief gap or pause after the song was natural and didn't need to be filled. It didn't need me going into overdrive, like I was the emcee, owning this thing.

For many years –
through good times
and bad; record
sales ups and downs
– I have said yes
when I meant no.

So what if for one or two seconds after everyone had finished singing there was silence, that it wasn't obvious to me who was running the show? What show, anyway? All I needed to do was to lean into that pause and remember that life isn't a performance; I don't have to entertain everyone all the time.

And I know about gaps. You've got to have gaps, quiet pauses – between songs and in life – otherwise it's just one long string of noise. And that few-second pause after 'Happy Birthday' was a good example of that – a silence that would have been followed by someone saying something like, 'Have a great day Craig', followed by some goodbyes and those little Zoom waves as we 'left the meeting'.

That image of everyone waiting patiently while I did my thing was now ingrained in my mind and it chipped away at me, and I knew that I had to take a look at why I'd behaved in that way. Why I hadn't just been able to receive the love that had come my way. Why I'd needed to take control. Why I'd needed to sing each person a five-minute, made-up riff, listing their attributes and making them feel like they were the most important person in my life at that moment, or always. The reality is that, while it was a really lovely gesture, I'd have been perfectly content with a short Zoom, a swim, time in the studio, dialling up some friends and family, a takeaway, a movie and some calm meditation. Chill and calm. I'd have taken that. So, why hadn't I? And then what had made me want to spend my birthday evening doing a TS5 set with all the technological problems of a virtual solo performance? No one would have minded. No one was *expecting* me to do anything. So, I asked myself why had I not even *thought* about or listened to what I wanted or needed to do on my birthday and why had I put everyone else first?

In my reading of the spiritual teachers, I'd come across some advice that resonated with me: in order to unpack ingrained patterns of behaviour, to get closer to your place of truth, you need to look to their origins, understand your motivations. To go back until you discover the source of them, to identify and unpack the reasons and places you think they originated from.

It didn't take me long to get to the bottom of my birthday behaviour – it came from years of outwardly masking who I really was and what I really wanted. Years of tucking my true self away, of being a people-pleaser to hide my insecurities. Years of being so forcefully out there pleasing everyone else, that even I was convinced that was who I was – the guy with the positive vibes, saying yes to everything, putting myself out there to make everyone else's day better. I was doing it as a defence mechanism against my imposter syndrome – I was terrified that people were going to discover who I 'really' was. That if I was ever truly and authentically my real self, they would stop liking or accepting me. They'd tell me I was a fake and that I'd some-how busked all this, busked writing all these songs.

Over time, I started to believe this myself and, for a while, this incorrect belief affected my decision-making. In Miami, I got so much love and positive reinforcement as this life-and-soul-of-the-party kind of guy – the performer, even in his own home – that I couldn't seem to rein it in when I needed to recharge, relax and receive. Instead, I'd reinforce the pattern I had got into, with even wilder displays of people-pleasing – throwing massive parties on nights when I just wanted to be at home alone with a movie; giving more of my time to people who just wanted the fun party guy and loved the attention I was giving them, but never gave anything back; doing more and more for everyone and always, however much I longed to say no, giving everything the loudest and brightest yes.

In the end, and as I painfully found out, this is unsustainable. For if we can't be true to ourselves, if we can't recognise ourselves in the day as the person we are when we lie down in bed at night, in those few moments before sleep, then what sort of truth are we holding?

YES

To some extent we all people-please. We can't go around in our own little bubbles, suiting ourselves all the time. Mostly, we tend to want to do the best for others and, of course, it's not all bad and it's not all doom and gloom. It's good and proper to want to be there for the people in your life and there are times when we all have to show up, even when we might not feel like it. And anyway, wanting to please people is a good thing; being empathetic, putting yourself out for others, meeting their needs – it's what helps the world go around. And it feels good when we can shine a little light into someone else's life; give them things we think they will like. It feels nice to be able to say yes, instead of no; it feels good when they thank you and compliment you.

You put yourself out – a little – and do what you have to do to make someone else feel good. But – and here's the difference – *you* have the capacity to say no when you feel you need to.

And until recently, that's been my problem. For years, I just wasn't able to say no. Take the Art Basel festival, one of the craziest weekends of the season in Miami Beach. The vibe is hectic, the parties dazzling with so many people coming through, so, one year, I decided that instead of doing a TS5 set at my place, I'd spend the weekend at other people's parties, enjoying myself and giving myself a break from being the performer. When I texted this to one of my mates, he called immediately.

You have the capacity to say no when you feel you need to.

'Come on, man,' he said. 'You've got to have a party at your place. It's going to be amazing. Everyone's hitting town tonight. I've got Leonardo DiCaprio coming through. P Diddy is coming through. Word is, they might come. You can't let *them* down.'

He continued reeling off names and I told myself, *say no, go and enjoy yourself, don't get busy. Nothing bad will happen if you say no.*

'Yes,' I said. 'Yes. OK. Let's do it. Get the word out. I'll get my set together, and leave the food and drink to me too.'

I had about three hours to get it all together. I couldn't get my usual security team so had to settle for some other guys they recommended. I called my housekeeper, Lourdes, to get in the tequila, champagne and food, and had Franco, who worked with her, load everything in, then went up to my studio to prepare the set.

Word got out mighty fast and, within a couple of hours, security had somehow let 200 people in (my apartment could just about take 60 if they were mostly on the balcony), all shoving their way to the food and drink. Most were people I didn't know and, while I sweated away doing my set, I could see them hoovering up the food and drink, disrespecting the place. When I clocked Leonardo DiCaprio and P Diddy in my living room, I could see that they weren't enjoying themselves either. As soon as I finished performing, the crowd appeared to leave as quickly as they'd arrived to move on to the next party and I was left with a ransacked apartment, now too exhausted to go out and enjoy the festival.

I'd heard myself say no, but I'd let myself get excited at the thought of being able to please my mate and impress a load of people I didn't even know. For some reason, instead of being able to hold my own, stick to what I wanted, through fear of disapproval, a fear of not being seen, I'd said yes. As this situation happened over and over again, I can see now that my life was one big self-compromise and, trust me, I was running one depleted and exhausted version of myself.

They say that from adversity comes strength and it turns out that there's some truth in that. Doing my back in and the resulting spiral into depression proved that to me because, when it became too painful and too much, I was *forced* to say no, *forced* to shut out the noise in my mind as I turned things down, *forced* to put my needs before the needs of others. And you know what? It didn't turn out so badly. The people around me understood what was happening. They got the memo. If I couldn't show up at something or meet a commitment because I wasn't able to move from my bed, they wished me well, told me to get better and that they'd see me soon. If I wasn't able to organise lavish surprises or presents for people to show how much I appreciated them, I either decided it could wait or not happen for now, or I found another, dialled-down way of showing my gratitude or love. Often, it was through a voice note or a WhatsApp – words from my heart, no bells or whistles and, trust me, when you are leaving messages, your words need to sound sincere and land, otherwise what's the point?

Leaving voice notes is a great way to listen to and limit yourself. You can't go on for too long, otherwise your listener will lose the will to live (if only I'd remembered that little piece of advice when I was on the birthday Zoom) and I found that if I was too gushy in my people-pleasing sort of way, listening back would make me cringe and feel embarrassed. After a while, I could feel myself calming down as I left messages, saying what I wanted or needed to say and then pressing 'send', with a feeling of quiet relief. And, more often than not, just the act of leaving a message was pleasing enough to the people around me.

Accepting that I wasn't able to be my 'normal' self, gave me space and time to reflect – to think about what I was like in certain situations, how I responded to people and different contexts, and how I could change things about myself so life was more comfortable for me and those around me.

Saying yes had been such a reflex action that 'no' seemed to be a word that just wasn't in my vocab. It felt like saying yes had been somehow wired into my DNA. But, when I thought about it, you have to be able to say no. A yes that means no isn't a yes. You don't need to be aggressive or on the defensive when you say no. You can say no with empathy and grace. You can say no calmly, without feeling you are letting people down. You can say no with good humour. Or you can just say no.

Since being forced not to say yes when my back was out and finding alternative ways of responding to people, I have made myself build on this. Though this has been hard for me, I have made some progress. Now, when I'm asked to do something that I don't want to do, I first take a breath and think about what I've been asked and how I would like to answer. Sometimes this can mean just putting the request into my mind, while the person asking me to do something and I have a chat. That way, if I am going to say no, it's not immediate or unfriendly in tone. Instead, it's a considered and thoughtful response. For a while, I found that I could say no to something specific – say an invite to a meal out – but then offered an alternative – *come to mine next week instead* – even if I knew that wasn't what I wanted. But as I realised that people weren't blacklisting me or never contacting me again when I turned down an invite, or – my greatest nightmare – telling me that I was a complete fraud and they'd always known that, I relaxed even that people-pleasing reflex.

Take the red carpet – I've always found that they make me anxious. It's beautiful to be part of, especially when I'm all dressed up, surrounded by the glitz and glam, but there's also something stressful with the photographers shouting, 'Craig, Craig, over here', the constant movement of so many people and the rush of back-to-back interviews, not even being able to hear the questions or catch a breath to answer. So now – and trust me, this has taken some time and finessing – when my current PA, Carly, who is absolutely invaluable, asks me if there is anything she can do to help make it easier, I'll say, 'If we can keep it moving, that's cool, but I need to be off that carpet as soon as we've done some photos and the key interviews.' If I get a feeling that that's not going to work, I've found it's easier to have her reply with, 'Thanks. It's so nice of you to invite Craig. He can't make the red carpet this time, but would love to still be at the event.'

At first, I'd come off the phone to Carly and would have to stop myself calling back and saying I made a mistake – *yes, yes, tell them I'll do the red carpet.* But what I came to realise was that no one said, 'Well, then hundreds of people will be let down by you and never listen to your music again.'

So I started to practise the power of no in other situations. I made myself say no when I meant no, instead of yes. If it was a friend and I'd told them I couldn't come to something or get them something or be somewhere, they said, 'Cool, no worries, talk soon.' And when, in 2019 at my Ibiza Rocks pool party, there was talk of me doing two performances in one day, I knew better. A few years before at Ronnie Scott's I'd said yes to doing two shows in one night. It had been a chance for me to showcase new songs from my album *Trust Me* with my band and introduce my special guest, Rita Ora, to perform our song 'Awkward'. Even though it was a great idea on paper and the audience had a wonderful time, it totally mashed my energy; I found myself depleted before the second show had even started, struggling to keep my vibe alive. So, this time, I heard myself politely say no and, as soon as the word no came out, I dug down, telling myself that I did not need to say yes. The organisers were completely respectful and the shows I did that summer ended up being the best season I'd ever had, the atmosphere electric and thrilling. In the end, the organisers were *grateful* to me for saying no, as they could see how two shows in one day would have been too awkward and the audience in the second show would have got a reduced performance from me. And being able to admit that I can't always say yes and still be on the top of my game was a huge relief.

And so I was learning. If I said no when I meant no, the world didn't tilt. And when I wanted to say yes, it came from a place of truth, and I turned up, showed up, feeling like I wanted to be there, fully present, no resentment simmering in a place I denied myself access to.

TRUST ME

In sharing this with you, I've realised that being a people-pleaser is interwoven with always having to exude a positive vibe – the two aren't unrelated – and that wearing that people-pleasing armour like it was impenetrable meant that, for so long, I tucked the true me away; the childhood me, the freer, more innocent,

By leaning into knowing yourself better, being true to yourself, saying no with empathy and grace, you too can start to breathe more easily into the real you.

uninhibited me. Saying yes for so many years, responding to the needs of those around me, taking the emotional temperature of the others in the room without checking mine, had taken its toll. Helping others, being mindful of others, giving to those around you, is a lovely thing. But needing to be needed isn't healthy; helping others at the sacrifice of your own needs is cumulatively just too tiring – like you are always being booked up, even when there aren't any available slots.

And you can't care for others if you aren't taking care of yourself. By leaning into knowing yourself better, being true to yourself, saying no with empathy and grace, you too can start to breathe more easily into the real you. And I promise, your world won't fall apart. Quite the opposite – it will get more balanced, more authentic and you'll feel better.

It takes work and time and, like in all the ways of external and internal change I'm experiencing, I'm still learning along the way and not always able to stay on course. Just last week, I said yes to going somewhere I'd rather not have gone. But once there, I thought about how next time I'd stick to my truth and how next year the event would go ahead without any major mishaps without me there. I didn't beat myself up over not staying true to my word, but accepted that was my decision and that was OK. Maybe, though, by recognising the impact being a people-pleaser has had on me – and others around me – and the ways I've been working on changing this and freeing myself from this, you can do the same and begin to readjust and change your patterns too.

And in case you were wondering, the Zoom birthday call didn't happen again. Instead, the following year, I made plans during the day and went to a friend's for supper in the evening. Perfect.

CHAPTER ELEVEN
Can't Be Messing Around

Since I've been trying to stop feeling responsible for making everyone else happy, straining to meet their needs, needing to be needed to the extent that I've squashed my own needs, I've had some space to think about what my personal and emotional boundaries are, the best way to communicate them to those around me and how to put them into effect. For me, this is about more than being able to say no. It's about feeling empowered and able to communicate my own needs and boundaries so that I feel comfortable and not compromised.

It turns out that a song I wrote back in 2000 had some insight into the importance of boundaries – at work, in life, with friends, family, neighbours and strangers. It took some time for me to put that sentiment into action – stop lying and start 'walking away' – but now I'm on my way, the days are just getting better and better.

My boundaries were tested recently when Colin's daughter, Emily, called to invite me to a birthday dinner for her brother, Jack. Jack and I are very close – I've known him since he was four years old and, since he left college, Colin has been mentoring him and, more recently, he has become the General Manager of JEM Music Group – Colin's management company – so now I also have a close working relationship with him.

But going out to eat, in a social setting, mostly with people I don't know, isn't straightforward for me and it's a boundary I've come to realise that I need to be in control of. While part of me is super-extrovert – like when I'm performing a TS5 set or on stage in front of thousands of people – the core of me is super-introverted. I find being around lots of people with various different energies all bouncing off each other a little too much, especially if I haven't got an exit plan in place. Stepping outside my comfort zone can be challenging and a lot of internal calculation goes on as I weigh up the range of discomfort/comfort in accepting an invitation.

Emily said, 'Please come for a bit, Craig. It will mean a lot to Jack.' While the old me would have said, 'Yes, count me in, can't wait,' before she'd have finished talking, now mindful of the new me, I instead took a moment to ask her how she was and, while I chatted, I worked through the invite in my mind a bit – the pause and the graceful 'no' ready to go. But, in this situation, I felt I'd be OK. The restaurant was so close to my home, I could have jumped ten times from my front door and landed in my seat and I wanted to be there to celebrate Jack's birthday. I also knew that Emily was keen for me to meet Sam, her new boyfriend, and I wanted to share and be included in her happiness and excitement at introducing him to her friends and family. Figuring that I'd be good to dip in and then, if I felt triggered, to dip out, I told her, 'Thanks for inviting me, count me in.'

Late in the afternoon on the day of the meal, Emily texted: 'Give me a call when you're here and I'll come down and meet you'. I appreciated this; she was looking out for me. I was already at the wobbly point of talking myself out of going. I was at home, comfortable and there was, as I could always justify, a litany of reasons as to why it wouldn't matter if I didn't show up: *they'll get on fine without me; better without me there; what if I get the attention that should be on Jack?; I'll disturb the vibe if I arrive late or leave midway; I can ask Jack, Emily and her boyfriend round here for a more intimate celebration sometime; do I need to go?; I've been recording this week, I need my rest time, my downtime, my alone time.* You get my vibe. I was looking for excuses – any reason not to go – my 'swerves', as I call them.

And then I looked outside. It was beautiful – that soft summer air, the light buttery as the late afternoon was turning – and, where I live, the vibe was homely and inviting, like a village. I wanted to be out there and so, before I could persuade myself otherwise, I put on some fresh clothes, picked up the gift I'd bought for Jack, took a deep breath, calming myself, and left the house, messaging Emily as I shut the front door.

Emily was outside the restaurant and together we went up to the room where she was hosting Jack's party. It was noisy in there and the vibes were high – and as I hugged Jack and said hi to his friends, my antennae picked up a bustling parallel table, around which sat another group of people celebrating a birthday.

Emily had made space at her end of the table and, as she introduced me to Sam, the drinks and starters were coming and, with the chaos of so many plates hitting the table, every-one talking, moving their drinks, leaning to the right or left as the waiters reached over their shoulders, for a moment I checked out, my discomfort meter on the rise. The room was too small for the noise everyone was creating and we were all shouting at each other to be heard. I don't know if that both-ers you, but having to project my voice to someone sitting right next to me and then having to concentrate so hard to hear their response, does me in. I did the best I could and, as I dipped in and out of the conversation, I looked over to Jack and could see he was having a good time. He gave me a thumbs up and I could tell in his smile that he was happy I was there. That's what mattered and, as starters were passed up and down the table, the smells of fresh cooking aromatic and delicious, I settled back and felt present in the moment.

As Sam and I talked – or shouted – out of the corner of my eye, I could see this one guy from the other table trying to get my attention. I'm used to this and I'm mostly happy to take selfies or be in photos or say hi, if I don't feel too interrupted, like if I'm in the middle of eating. He was the entertainment for the table next to us. Cradling a guitar in his arms, he started singing, his eyes locked on me. His vibe was cool, laid back and he sounded good. I looked away, while conscious of needing to keep him in sight.

He moved to our table, coasting towards me – smiling, singing beautifully – and everyone from his table had turned to look, expectation filling the air. I told myself: *be calm, he's just singing.* But as he came nearer, the atmosphere changed and, within a heartbeat, I knew what was coming. And in that same moment, I knew what I didn't want to, and couldn't, do. My boundary was about to be compromised and the new me wasn't going to let that happen.

There are times when you can't stop what's happening and explain yourself. I didn't want to sing, I didn't want to *perform.* I looked at Emily, who was eyeing the guitarist now, with a thousand-yard please-don't-try-it stare and, as the guy closed in, I turned to her and said as quietly as I could, 'I've gotta dip,' and she said, 'Go Craig, it's cool.' So, before the guy with the guitar could get any closer and give me a cue to take over,

My boundary was about to be compromised and the new me wasn't going to let that happen.

I got up, went around to the other side of the table to Jack, leaned down and said, 'I'm just going to the toilet.'

He knew that move of mine, but, as always, he had my back. He said, 'Thanks for coming man,' and I knew he was good with it. This all happened within a few seconds and, as the guy kept singing, his gaze boring a hole in my back, I left the room and flew down the stairs. As I stepped into the warm night air, I took a deep breath to steady myself. Back home, I messaged Jack and Emily to thank them for looking out for me and asked them to suggest a time to come round, with Sam, for a meal at mine.

Later, I thought about what had gone down and how I'd not given into the pressure of performing, of doing something that crossed my boundary. Not wanting to people-please is one thing, but being a party pooper is another. So, instead,

I'd left. Probably, on reflection, I should have signalled a 'no thanks, man'. *Communicated* my boundary. I wish I'd had the inner confidence to be able to say, 'You carry on and I'll watch and appreciate your singing,' and to have stayed at the meal with Jack and Emily, eaten well and gone home having had a good evening out with the people I love.

Was the singer unhappy in the moment? So what if he was? I know now that I can't please all of the people all of the time. While, before my back went and I was forced to change my yes/no ratio, I would have found his unhappiness because of my behaviour, even if for a moment, *mortifying*, now, as Obama said the night before the 2016 US Presidential election: *no matter what happens, the sun will rise in the morning*, I know that I'd have woken up the next morning and things would have carried on.

Just because I've only recently been able to set healthy boundaries in my adult life, it doesn't mean I didn't know what boundaries were growing up. I vividly remember one particular situation when my dad taught me the importance of setting clear boundaries. Dad and I went 'into business' together when I was 14 and *obsessed* with speakers. I needed to earn some money to be able to afford more equipment. So, always the optimistic entrepreneur, along with selling my mixtapes around the neighbourhood and my chocolate before morning break, I agreed to make a kid at school some custom speakers for £200.

I asked my dad, who was an ace carpenter, to help me make them. I'd spent many Saturday afternoons with him as he built kitchens and he'd slip me a fiver or tenner every so often for fetching him tools or sweeping up, and that would go towards tapes and hi-fi stuff. So when it came to making some custom, bespoke speakers, I felt he'd be down with it. 'Sure,' he said. 'I've got the wood and the paint, you buy the equipment and we'll be good to go.'

The next Sunday we got to work in my grandma's garden. I watched as my dad mitred the side of the wood and fashioned it until we'd built a box emulating what I'd seen in shops. I didn't exactly *know* how to build a speaker, but I did know about the component parts: the stack, the high tower, the cone and the woofer, the shock absorbers, the top tweeters; how we needed to drill on the little black grille at the front and make a separate part for the mid-range. We worked on this together, the sun shining down into my grandma's small front garden.

'OK,' Dad said, as we stepped back to admire our handi-work, as the last coat of black matt paint was drying, 'what's the plan? What are we doing with them?'

I looked at him proudly and said, 'I'm selling them, Dad. This kid in my class, Wesley, wants to buy them. He's paying me £200 for the two.'

Dad looked at me and said, 'OK, cool. We're going to split it, right? 50:50.'

Wow. I'd assumed the profit would be all mine, that Dad had done this out of the kindness of his heart. It was awkward for a few seconds as I stared at the ground. But when I thought about how much time and work he'd put in, I realised, *no, he's right. This is business and why should I keep all the profit?*

I looked at him. 'Sure, Dad,' I said. 'Let me get the cash from Wesley and we'll settle up next week.'

I'd like to think that, since then, I've always been fair when it comes to professional boundaries, always respecting the work that others put in. And, for once, it was nice for *me* to slip my dad some cash.

YOU KNOW WHAT

This is how I visualise boundaries now: if you're living in a house with a garden and I'm living next door with the same and we haven't got a fence up, there's no way of knowing where my garden ends and yours begins. Without some sort of demarcation, how do I know if I'm stepping on your grass or you're watering my plants? In reality, we might get on really well and it may not bother either of us, but, equally, you may be growing new seedlings and not want me trampling over them and I may have already tended my plants and your water may oversaturate them.

To solve this, we put up a fence – a visible marker between our properties – and then we know what's what. The boundaries are set. If I then want you to come into my garden, I can invite you. And the same goes for you inviting me into yours. We know – because we can *see* – where the limits are and it's up to us to negotiate around them.

But what if we're good friends, always pleased to see each other, but I love hugging and you don't like hugging or being hugged? Every time I see you, I lean in for a great big embrace, holding you to me for a moment or two. And every time I do that, inside you scream: *no, don't hug me, get off, get away, can't you* see, *don't you* know, *that I don't like being touched?* The problem here is that I *can't* see – there's no fence around your physical space indicating that you don't want to be hugged and you are far too polite to recoil or push me away.

That's the difficulty with our personal and emotional boundaries. They're largely invisible and, unless we're able to make it clear to others what we do and don't accept in their behaviour towards us, we may suffer in silence. Recognising our own boundaries can be straightforward for some – another friend, without any personal grief or difficulty, may be able to tell me, 'Hey Craig, do you mind not hugging me every time we see each other? Nothing personal, I just don't like it.' Hearing that would be fine. Being me, for a while after, I'd be cross with myself that I hadn't picked that up and that you might have thought badly of me for not being aware of it, but then I'd also realise this wasn't about me and I'd totally respect you for having told me. And I'd change my behaviour. On seeing you the next time and forever after that, I'd stop invading your personal space, squashing you up against me in one of my heartfelt bear hugs and be glad you'd been able to tell me.

To some degree or other, all of us have boundaries that go unsaid – things we won't stand for, like the way we're spoken to or being humiliated; things we don't want to do; situations we don't want to put ourselves in; work we won't take on. But, like me, you may not recognise or be able to address your own other significant boundaries, because you worry that, if you give voice to things that make you feel uncomfortable, people will think badly of you or turn away from you.

There are still two versions of myself and sometimes I struggle with that. For me, there's the performer – it's easy for this version of myself to make everyone happy, break into song, have a few laughs about it after; and then there's the other version of me that's exploring my boundaries and learning to put them into practice. But I can feel lost between both versions. Torn. Had I made the situation at Jack's birthday meal into one big, unnecessary, egotistical drama? Why did it have to be about me? I could've just gone with the flow, hit a few notes, and then we could have all got back to where we'd been before the guy started playing his guitar with me as his target.

Boundary setting isn't easy and this situation gave me a lot to think about. What I was sure about was that the defining reason I had left the restaurant was because of the feeling I was getting from the situation. My boundaries were about to be crossed and I didn't like that feeling. And if I can't control the external element – I couldn't change the fact that the guy wanted me to sing – or can't change what's going on, I can be true to my own emotional and physical boundaries and do what feels right for me to navigate through uncomfortable situations.

If you struggle with putting boundaries in place, going to the root cause can help give you perspective on where something is coming from. You might have grown up in a family where you had to put all your needs to one side and accommodate those of others around you, and that pattern is ingrained in you. Or, like me, later, you might have buried your own needs in order to please others around you. Whatever the reason, if you try to drill down, that can give you a foundation on which to build upwards.

I've found that one way of setting boundaries is by practising what I might say if the scenario were to play out. And like practising a new song that I've just written, the words not yet fully locked in my mind in a way that I'd be ready to perform them perfectly on stage, so I practise out loud, over and over again, until the words flow effortlessly from my mouth. Practising your responses out loud is a great way of feeling empowered when/if the scenario arises, as you know you've rehearsed this. You've memorised your lines, you know the script and you know your character in the movie of your life is the one who has to speak up and honour their truth confidently and not buckle when faced with resistance.

Knowing our boundaries and being able to communicate effectively so that we can set them is, in my opinion, crucial to living a more harmonious life. It makes things clearer for ourselves and others, and generally will result in more straightforward and hassle-free interactions. But what if your boundaries make others uncomfortable? Remember what happened when my friends sang me 'Happy Birthday' – I so couldn't cope, I turned it back on them, with a force that was almost vengeful. It was, as was so much about the way I behaved, also about control. That made me reflect on that side of my behaviour, which I realised may have been causing boundaries that were difficult for others, and unnecessary for me too.

For many years, I felt unworthy of receiving from those around me, uncomfortable when being given a gift or something unexpected. This was all tangled up in a complicated mixture of feeling as though I wasn't deserving, not wanting to feel I was an imposition on anyone and needing to be in control of what was happening. It was easier for me to give, give, give. I wanted to be known for being so generous, so thoughtful, so kind, so *giving*. I also felt in control when I gave a gift. When someone else gave me something, I felt as if I was losing that control and that I had to give more to compensate.

In the past, if a friend gave me a present for my birthday, instead of opening it and receiving it with good grace, I'd go into an overdrive of 'thank you's, put it to one side and give them something in return. I'd bombard them with gratitude and then find something to give to them. I see now that I was taking the joy of giving from them.

It's taken me a while, but I'm getting better at receiving. When a friend came round the other day and bought me some handmade chocolates, instead of a volley of *you shouldn't have, I don't need anything, you don't need to bring me anything* – as if they'd bought me the elixir of life itself – this time, I took a second or two and said: 'That's so lovely of you. They look gorgeous, I'll really enjoy them. Thank you.'

The smile on my friend's face said it all. In lifting that boundary, in showing my gratitude and receiving the gift with the love and gentleness and kindness she'd put into giving it, I'd freed us both up from my control.

WHEN YOU KNOW WHAT LOVE IS

Trust me, being able to set your boundaries and live with them – hopefully without any great kickback (even if there is initially, know that this will settle) – will confirm your own sense of self-worth. You must value yourself for who you are. Because if you're confident and robust enough to set a limit

You must value yourself for who you are.

on what you agree to in your work and personal life, then this makes things much more straightforward, both for you and for others. It prevents resentment, lying, mixed messages and messed-up communication.

Setting healthy boundaries with, say, a colleague at work can be less complicated than setting them with those we love. I know that I've often found it so much easier to accept whatever it is that's threatening to cross my boundary – or has already – rather than making things awkward with those closest to me, even if it's created unnecessary tension or hurt for me.

Since working on setting my boundaries, every time that I've let something slide and crossed my own boundaries, I get instant feedback, a cascading feeling of self-betrayal and a tightening of the muscles around my heart, which always lets me know that I have let myself down.

I had this experience in 2021, while filming Simon Cowell's TV music show *Walk the Line*, in which the winner had the chance to take home £500,000 in prize money. Each week, the winner of the show bet on themselves based on their performance to take the leap of faith – to walk the line to go up against new contestants the following night, or cash in on smaller sums.

Before filming each show, there'd be a debrief from the night before and preparation on what was coming up that night. Ben, one of the producers, would come into my dressing room and we'd chat things through, so that I was prepared and had a vibe on the new contestants who were going to challenge the winner of the previous show for the prize money.

On the third afternoon of filming, Colin and Jack happened to be in my dressing room when Ben came in for our chat. Ben started to show me short teasers of the upcoming artists and then, as he had on the previous days, asked me what my thoughts were about them. Before I could say anything, Colin jumped in and proceeded to give his opinion of the first artist. I leaned in and listened, and put his interruption down to us all being excited in the moment. After all, being on this show was intoxicating and we were all feeling the thrill of it. But, as the same thing happened for each of the next four artists, I felt both cross at the fact that Colin was stepping over my boundaries and deflated that I wasn't speaking up. I was aware that I didn't want to burst out and say something I would regret in the moment, so, when we had a break, I left the room, went into a nearby bathroom, walked into a cubicle and sat down on the seat, dejected and flat. On the one hand, I felt like I wanted to scream and, on the other, like I wanted to cry. I felt as though Colin was talking for me because my opinion didn't count, that I was the imposter in this situation, not really worthy of being the actual judge I'd been appointed to be. Even, in a calmer moment, that Colin was doing this so that Ben didn't discover the fraud that I was.

After a few deep breaths, I calmed myself down, quietened the noise going on inside me, and thought: *No. No one needs to speak for me.* I knew it couldn't be left to fester as that would mash up my vibes for the show.

Just as I was gathering my last thoughts, as if on cue, Colin came into the bathroom and knocked on the cubicle door.

'All OK in there, Craig?' he asked and, in that moment, I knew that I had two choices: I was either going to say, 'All good Col, be out in a minute' and do nothing, betraying myself just to keep things cool and safe; or I was going to step out of the cubicle and my comfort zone and have a raw, honest conversation about how Colin had made me feel in that dressing room.

In my new iteration of understanding and attempting to set my boundaries, there was really only one option. And because I have so much love for Colin, and an equal amount for myself, I had to deal with this in the here and now. Otherwise, as I knew only too well from past behaviour, a piece of me would have broken off and been filed in the 'I-accept-this-type-of-behaviour-and-it's-OK-with-me' drawer.

Taking a big breath, I stepped out of the cubicle and asked Colin to come outside to a small, quiet corner of the corridor.

I wanted to explain how his continuous interrupting had made me feel and how, unconsciously, he wasn't respecting my boundaries. This was big for me, as pretty much from the moment I met him, I've always had a father–son relationship with Colin. But I was no longer 18 and, as a grown man, in this moment, I needed to be real and speak to the situation.

And you know what? Something wonderful happened – something that I didn't expect. As I explained how I was feeling and watched his expression as my words landed, I could feel how deeply connected and present Colin was, tuned into my every word. I could feel his heart open up as he realised how his actions were affecting me and he immediately told me he was genuinely sorry he had made me feel that way.

As Colin apologised, I gave space for him to speak, rather than, as I would have done in the past, rushing in to fill any of the awkward gaps. I had to keep that people-pleasing mechanism at bay for the conversation to have an impact. And it turned into a beautiful moment where I felt seen and, for Colin, it was an opportunity for quiet reflection to see how his unconscious actions had affected me. We hugged it out, said that we loved each other and I walked back into the dressing room feeling lighter, more present, knowing that I had made a deep connection with Colin and had retrieved part of my soul for all the other times I hadn't spoken up. Colin later told me that he felt emotional as he realised that I needed to do things my way and, to him, it was as though his son was finally leaving home.

When you love someone and that person is so closely involved in your life, it can make things seem harder to deal with, especially if you've made them a parental figure, as I had done in the early days of my career with Colin. As the wide-eyed teenager about to enter the uncharted territory of the music business, Colin had taken on the role of guiding me through it, like an adoptive parent. But, as with any healthy parent–child relationship, as the child grows, so too do certain aspects of the relationship, which, as I have found, is actually even more beautiful as so many parts of the connection are deeper and more evenly balanced.

As Ben continued briefing me on that evening's acts and I gave him my thoughts and insights, I could feel Colin listening and paying attention to what I had to say. In between my words, I could hear myself settle and knew that, because I'd had the strength to voice this boundary issue with him, Colin and I were entering an even more profound and beautiful place in our 22 years together.

Knowing and setting your boundaries takes courage. But, trust me, once you voice it – as I did with Colin, calmly, clearly and with conviction – say it and mean it, and start putting it into practice, you'll find it holds a powerful energetic vibe. And even if you get some kickback, once you've voiced it, you will be able to dig deeper than you think and stick to it. It's taken me years to put this into practice myself, but there's plenty of respect in the room once your boundaries have been communicated.

CHAPTER TWELVE

Stop, Look, Listen

When I moved into my new home, one of the features I appreciated was a small car parking space literally outside my front door. I live in a narrow, cobbled road, so it was useful for off-street parking, but each time I came in from being outside, I began to see images of this space that didn't involve a steel-grey hard floor, or a car. This often happens to me – a vision begins to take shape in my mind and, over time, it transforms itself into a new reality. I paused to consider what it was that I was imagining. I don't know about you, but, for me, if something is in my mind and takes on new forms and shapes, there comes a time when I have to act on it. So, I set to work, first painting the floor black, which made the space look a whole lot nicer and then, as I saw how the ivy was growing around the trellis on the wall, I saw green and I saw water and I saw calm and then I saw a wheel of bright, happy colour.

Rather than rushing in and hiring contractors to do this all for me, I took my time. There was, I told myself, no rush. I got some artificial grass to lay over the shiny-black floor and applied for a permit to park my car outside. With the car no longer in sight, it seemed that my garage was no longer my garage and, once that became clear in my mind and a reality in practice, this opened up the floodgates to creativity.

Growing up in our council flat in Southampton, we'd had a small balcony, home to my BMX and some plastic flowers and plants, but the outside space was communal and mostly concrete, the small patch of grass not easily accessible from our flat. We looked out over other flats, car parking spaces and a kind of unevenly paved yard. My nan, though, had a small garden and helping her water it – that tin watering can seemed so *heavy* as she helped me hold it over the plants – seeing the way she tended and cared for it and how much joy it gave her, it had always been my ambition to, one day, have my own outside space.

In Miami, while I'd had a gorgeous balcony overlooking the bay – the joy that view gave me was unparalleled – I'd still never had a garden of my own, since I'd been living mostly in hotels or serviced apartments, or been on tour, never anywhere long enough to cultivate anything. In fact, I'd never grown a thing. I didn't know how to and, to be honest, had never really thought about it. If I wanted some flowers, I'd go to the florist; if I wanted some herbs, I'd go to the supermarket.

Do you remember that guy who went viral in September 2020, after his 60p basil plant from Morrisons grew and grew into a giant, beautiful, fresh-smelling basil fest, lasting over a year? If, like me, you don't think you can do it, next time you go out, look upwards at other people's balconies and around you at their front gardens – the array of variety, colour and love that goes into growing and creating beautiful flowers and shrubs is something breathtaking and inspiring. I realise now that, if you want to cultivate plants or grow flowers, you just need a patch of grass or a balcony – or even a window box or some space on the floor – some time, some patience and the will to make your plants or flowers bloom.

In Miami, there'd been palm trees everywhere and I'd loved that tropical feel. So I looked into getting a couple of fake ones on Amazon – Prime, so they'd arrive the next day. Before I pressed 'Buy now', I showed the picture to Gina, telling her, 'Look! We are going to have palm trees!'

'Craig,' she said, in her gently patient way, that I knew meant something was coming, 'wait. Those trees look so far from any tropical tree I've ever seen, we need to get *real*.' She tapped something into her phone and held it up, smiling.

'This is more like it,' she said and showed me some photos from back home in the Philippines – lush and bountiful shrubs, trees and plants, that made me see instantly that fake palm trees in a small former-garage were not the way forward.

'We might not be able to get this *exactly*,' she said, 'so let's do the next best thing. Come to the garden centre with me and we can pick out some real plants.'

This was during one of the coronavirus lockdowns, but once the restrictions were lifted, we did just that. And so did everyone else, it seemed. We queued up for what seemed like a lifetime, but the mood was happy and relaxed. As I'd never been to a garden centre before, I was overwhelmed by the range and variety of plants on offer; it was as if the plants were holding the space, life bursting forth everywhere we looked and, as we chose pots and seeds and bulbs and flowers and, yes, a couple of real trees, I felt closer to the real earth than I ever had before.

Back home, Gina and I got to work. As we got digging and planting, I felt grounded, literally, with my hands in the earth, the soil under my fingernails. And when I was out there, I felt like I was slowing down. I was really seeing things – stopping one morning to watch a spider weave its web, it blew my mind to see how intricately every single part was created, so precisely. I don't know if you've ever actually watched how a spider does it – the way it constructs the shape of its web, the way it has to stop for a rest every so often, the way the web gleams when it's finished – and come to understand that everything has its place.

Over the next few months, I had beautiful plants growing. Nature was starting to take over my old, grey garage.

Buds were sprouting open and, by mid-summer, flowers were bursting through. Seeds had dispersed into my artificial grass and real grass grew up in tufts in some places. Birds came in to visit. Mice came in to take the feed I'd left out for the birds (though, after a while, with total respect to the mice that were just doing their thing, I had to rehouse them).

When my basil and mint and oregano grew and there was enough for me to use in my cooking – who I am trying to kid, Gina's cooking – it was the best feeling ever. Have you ever picked a mint leaf, rolled it between your fingers and smelled it? It's so *fresh*. And then when you put it in hot water for a mint tea, there's nothing like knowing you've grown it, you've tended it, you've had the patience and put in the care. Trust me, you won't stop going on about it, handing visitors a cup of it and watching as they take a sip, telling them – pretty much yelling at them – 'That's the best cup of mint tea *ever*, isn't it? Taste it, really *taste* it.' And then, 'I grew that. I *grew* that!'

It was the same with the lavender; the aroma was off the scale. And watching the bees come to take their fill of pollen was nothing short of joyful. And as for the root ginger that Gina grew from a small piece she'd bought from the supermarket … you've never seen anything like it, a three-foot plant of wonder.

From the appreciation of starting something and seeing it through, to the pleasure of the reds and the oranges, the violets and the lavenders that made me smile every time I walked past or sat on the tiny bench in my 3-metre by 3-metre garden, I felt blessed by the profound power of nature, out there doing her stuff, with no fuss or fanfare, taking her own sweet time.

But it didn't happen overnight. Flowers will bloom when they're ready and you can't hurry things along by plying plants with more water or more food. I'd come to feel a great respect for the ebb and flow of life – an understanding that, in the natural cycle of the seasons, there's a time for blooming and positive moments and a time for hibernation, when it all closes down. To be honest, I'd never really thought about this, but, once I listened in, I saw that pausing helps us slow down. And slowing down, stilling our minds and bodies, can be good for us in so many ways.

Just as I'd experienced when 'stepping out' of the scene at the end of my '7 Days' video, it was like I was being given subconscious clues of how life actually plays out and, if I was to tune into the finer details, I could see that adjusting how I interacted with it would have a huge impact. At the time, it just felt like a coincidence that one of my favourite movies (*Groundhog Day*) would combine with my song like this in such a life-affirming moment, but I've come to realise that it wasn't a coincidence, but rather subtle guidance dressed up in the form an R&B music video.

By being able to *see* repeating patterns in my own 'life' movie, I was then able to *see* if I liked the storyline that was playing out. If I didn't like any parts of it, I had the chance to make some changes that could produce different, more positive outcomes in the future. You know the type of scenario – seeing the same person at work who says the same thing that always triggers you, trying to mash up your good vibes, yet it keeps happening again and again. Noticing the storyline that keeps repeating is the first step. Next – and this is my favourite part – is to realise that you're the co-director and the lead star in your own movie. You've cast some amazing extras who aren't breaking character, but, as the co-director, you can change the way you relate to them and rewrite the storyline in real time by using the power of the pause. Simply put, this just means finding a moment when you give yourself a chance to slow down and reflect on the situation. It's from this vantage point that changes to the script can be made before jumping back into the scene. This might look like

With the power of the pause comes patience and a way of looking into your life and rhythms and routines with a bit of distance.

avoiding that work colleague completely, or maybe it's telling them how you feel; maybe it's just leaving that environment entirely and loving yourself. The most important thing to remember is that you are the co-director and can flip the script when you want to. I know that it can seem easier said than done, but seeing life as 'all a movie', with you as the lead star, returns the power to you to make subtle or huge changes to how you participate in the story.

With the power of the pause comes patience and a way of looking into your life and rhythms and routines with a bit of distance. You have time to think, time to stop, time to reconsider. You have distance between yourself and the frantic dash of everyday life; you have distance between yourself and the demands that you and others place upon you.

MEANT TO BE

They say that if you give out the right energy to the universe, in a calm, patient and even way, something will come back and surprise you when you least expect it and, during this time of patience and rebirth, it did.

There's a Yiddish word 'Beshert', which means 'destiny', that I always use when something magical aligns in my life.

And on one wet Wednesday afternoon, while recording in my home studio, I was about to experience it. That morning,

I'd woken up with a bit of a sore throat and, even though I didn't have any solid plans for the day, I did want to do some recording in my studio, so I told myself that I'd get through it and that no sore throat was going to stop me. So, after squeezing a whole lemon, which I'd freshly picked from my garden, into my tea and stirring in a spoon of honey, I walked upstairs to my studio and got to it. Instead of being in my normal effortless flow, I found myself frustrated by the constant pain I felt every time I opened my mouth to sing. The more I pushed to get the notes out, the more painful my throat became, but, once again, I told myself that a song had to get done today and that was that.

Determined to get something down, I carried on. But, as the day wore on, I was feeling more and more frustrated at the vocals not sounding right and irritated every time I swallowed. Despite my insistence, willing to make it work, rather than anything productive happening, I ended up fixed to my computer screen, my cup now swimming with lemon pips and a throat red raw from all the singing.

It was at this point that I noticed a small photo on my shelf with the words 'Love Yourself' displayed on it, which I'd printed out a few days before and framed as a little reminder to slow down and check in from time to time. In this moment it seemed to be speaking to me loud and clear, and I certainly wasn't loving the way my throat was feeling, nor the frustration that I didn't have a finished song. So, leaving my cup half full, I turned off the computer, went back downstairs, jumped on the sofa and threw on one of my favourite movies, *Soul*.

As I relaxed and enjoyed the movie, I noticed my throat had started to ease off and my good vibes were returning. As it got nearer the end of the movie, there's a part where one of the characters – Joe Gardner – plays the piano in a beautiful reflective moment and he sees the real meaning of life. This moment always seems to get me in my feels and it was at this point that my phone pinged and I saw that I'd received a message. It was from rapper KSI.

'Yo, Craig, hope you're good bro! Been a fan of your music for a long time now and I've been working on a song called "Really Love" and wanted to reach out to see if you were down for jumping on it with me?'

I mean, talk about divine timing. So I went upstairs, threw the song on, which I loved, and replied, 'I'm down my bro, this tune is fire. It'd be my pleasure.'

One thing led to another and, a few weeks later, we shot a video, released the single and it soared up the charts straight into number two, which was KSI's highest entry at that time. It was as if in taking a moment away from my studio, away from constantly trying to force the melody out with sheer grit and determination, that there – right there in the moment of surrender – it was 'Beshert' and, by not forcing the situation, I was able to see that it really *was* love that had my best interests at heart.

By pausing, stopping even, from time to time, taking stock, thinking slowly and with space between my thoughts, I've now realised that's when my creativity flows back in. I loved working with KSI and his crew and, as my creativity flowed and my inner belief in myself was growing, it was like this new lease of life took hold and I felt this little ripple in the wave, and the wave started to build. All of a sudden, I could feel that I was freeing myself up – like this lightness had taken shape inside me – and, as Covid restrictions lifted, I thought: *I need to make some changes to the way in which I've been working. Before launching back into studio work, I need to think about how things might go forward in the new moments of freedom we're getting and how I can best put these new feelings of creativity into practice.*

My studio routine had always been rigid: I would go into the studio three or four times a week, from 2 to 8pm. It will come as no surprise to you that I like routine – it suits my need to be in control, to know where I am. I'd always insisted on sticking to those hours, worried that if we went on longer, loosened the reins, I wouldn't get a good night's sleep or be productive the next day.

One day, as my barber, Sharo, was cutting my hair, I played him one of the songs I'd recorded the day before in my allotted 2–8pm timeslot.

'Craig,' he said, 'this tune is *fire*. Imagine, if you'd carried on last night, what else you could have created. Sounded like you were really on a roll. Ever thought of recording way into the night?'

I couldn't answer. Having time to think and recalibrate as he continued making the fade seamless on the back of my head, I was like, why? Why have I always tried to control this situation? Why do I need to finish dead on 8pm? I mean, structure works to a certain degree, but I was taking it to the limit for no reason. This made me really start to question my whole approach. I was so regimented that, if we were in the middle of something and it was 7.30pm, internally I'd be going: *time to wrap up, shut this down, you've got half an hour to pack up and get out of here.* It didn't matter if we were on to something good or the vibe was right, I'd be sticking to that 8pm cab outside the studio, no matter what. But Sharo now had me questioning this.

We all need to shake things up from time to time. Working from home during lockdown gave many of us a new and sometimes refreshing perspective that it's not always necessary to be in an office or, in my case, the studio. You might have

We all need to
shake things up
from time to time.

experienced this too – changing your daily routine, you might have been able to add in that extra walk or more time with your loved ones. And maybe it made your working life easier and you've tried to do things differently as things go back to 'normal'. Even if your work isn't flexible and you have to be on site or you work shifts, that doesn't mean you can't make changes to your priorities – it's worth pausing now to think about what could make your days flow better.

You know what I'm going to say: write it down. Write it down and let the thoughts that hit the page settle in you and take shape and, before long, if you're anything like me, this will lead to some new ways of seeing things. The pause happens between writing things down and putting something new into action. There may be no immediate hurry, the changes more long-term, but, as soon as you start to feel change is needed, get your thoughts, however unformed at first, down on the page or into your phone – somewhere you can see them in black and white.

This process can work for big and small things; logistical issues or bigger lifestyle changes. If your working hours compromise time with your family or time you want to spend playing sport or pursuing your passion, take a moment to consider what you'd ideally like, within reason – I don't mean winning the lottery or stumbling on some precious treasure, but you could still give it a go – and then write it down. Start the narrative and let it build. The solutions will follow.

OBVIOUS

Having realised that I was being too rigid in my inelastic studio timetable, I started to think about what might work better and jotted down some ideas. First, the 2pm start. Might that change? I thought about it for a few days, more aware of my routines and pattern from waking up to 1pm, which is when I'd be getting ready to leave for the studio. I decided that this was the best time, that starting then suited my rhythm and meant I could take care of other things in the mornings. It was comfortable for all sorts of reasons and meant members of my crew could do other things they needed to do before we set to work. The 2pm start was staying.

Then I asked myself: *What would it be like if we didn't have the 8pm cut-off?* The studio is a 30-minute journey from my place and I'd been relying on a cab to take me and bring me home. What, I wondered, if I drove myself there and back so I had the freedom to come and go when I wanted? Was there anything else about the set-up that I needed to address? Yes – the rest of the team's needs: would they appreciate an element of flexibility?

Giving voice to these questions was so helpful. Seeing my concerns written down on the page in front of me, I was able to let them settle and, slowly – the pause again, there was no hurry in this – I was able to work things out in my mind and implement some changes.

This is what I came to see: we could work for three days a week, starting at 2pm without any rigid cut-off; I could drive myself to and from the studio; and so that I wasn't being rigid about not being rigid, we could try this out for a time and see if it suited us all.

Let's see where it goes, I told myself and, wow, as soon as we were able to return to the studio, let me tell you, it went. Everyone involved was on board to give it a go, from Barry Burt (my A&R man), who was so happy that I'd given myself permission to be more flexible, to Carly who was ready to stockpile Cadbury's Marvellous Creation chocolate bars for the late-night stint. This all gave me a big boost – and I'm not just talking the chocolate kind; from the beginning, the vibe was right. And the changes worked.

When I came back to London, I didn't have a car, so I got used to getting lifts to and from the studio. I'd lost a bit of confidence driving on the left-hand side of the road so it was only recently, when I moved into my home, that I'd bought a Mini Cooper – not quite a Ferrari in style, but just as nifty and nippy.

So, driving myself to the studio was a jump and I loved it. I felt free; like I was back in control, stripped back, a return to who I was all those years ago in Southampton in my little Peugeot 206. If I wanted to go left for no reason, make a right, take a wrong turn, I could do it. It honestly felt like I was calling in a piece of my soul that had gone missing. It may seem like madness to you, but I was excited just filling up the car with petrol, thrilled to see the sunrise on one or two occasions, to take a detour and drive through town. Who knew that at 5am the streets of London belong to foxes? And the best times were when, on the way home, I'd put on the music we'd been recording in the studio and sing along at the top of my voice, all the way home. Just like the old 'Rewind' days with the Artful Dodger.

Working in this way was immediately freeing and cathartic for my music. I felt like I was writing some of the best tunes. I was working more regularly with Mike Brainchild, a talented producer whose energy and vibe is not only pitch-perfect for making great music together, but the laughs and jokes that we have every time only adds to the enjoyment of the new friendship we've formed.

It feels like the old days, back when Mark Hill and I were riffing off each other and coming up with 'Fill Me In' and '7 Days' well into the night. That feeling of music flowing through me has come back, and I'm responding by writing it down, keeping on doing my thing, keeping on having fun and, as soon as I get home from the sessions, I love nothing more than sending Colin, Jack and Barry the demos, knowing how excited they are when they listen to them first thing on waking up.

By pausing to think if the rigid timetable vibe was working, I had come to understand that it wasn't. When we started working with the new, flexible timetable, I realised there was no box I was putting myself in and this was manageable three days a week for us all. I felt creatively free to flow. And being more willing to relinquish my iron grip on control, I was able to see things in other areas of my life more flexibly too. For a few weeks, I was on a real high, making the best music that I could and then a situation came up that put all my new people-pleasing, boundary-setting, pause-embracing practices into place.

Towards the end of 2020, Colin got a call from Fred Gibson, also known as Fred Again, a multitalented guy who's worked with loads of artists, including Ed Sheeran. Fred won Producer of the Year at the 2020 BRITs and he was interested in me doing something with Kurupt FM again, who he was now producing.

I've got so much love for Kurupt FM – they have this beautiful way of depicting the garage scene and everyday life in such an accurate, relatable way and they never break character; they're great performers. Because I love the idea of things coming around again – the full-circle moment – this ticked all the boxes for me. The plan was to do a recording with them until 6pm and then go back to my studio to do my session with Mike. I was pretty hyped when Colin ran this by me, but something was nagging at me, so, before agreeing to it, I told him that it sounded great, but that I needed to live with it for a moment and I'd call him back to confirm.

So I just sat with it for a bit. There was this inner dialogue that was happening – the part of me that was hyped about this coming about and the fact that I could get two songs in one day from both sessions. When I thought about the opportunity, it excited me to be putting myself out there to make it all happen. However, the new, more-aware me was taking that pause – in going to the Kurupt FM session, I'd be working on something that might need to go over the allotted time and, if I knew I had to be back at my studio, with people waiting for me, I'd have boxed myself in and, for some time near the end, not really be fully present in either space.

And the me that's learning leaned into that pause and thought: *What's the feeling going to be like?* I sat with that for a bit. *What's the* feeling *you're going to get when it hits 6pm and you haven't finished that first track, but you have to dip out? What's the* feeling *you're going to get at 5pm when you know you've only got an hour and you're starting to look at the time as opposed to it just flowing and knowing there's no boundary? What's that* feeling *going to be like?*

And that feeling felt restricted. It felt tight and constrained. It felt like a red flag that my creativity would be compromised. That's what I had to sit with; I needed to pause for a moment.

And I decided that having two sessions in one day wasn't going to happen. It wasn't the right vibe. For me, that was a huge step in the direction of being able to have the pause, to hold it. And this feeling rose up in me and I knew I had to say no to doing both – to just commit to one session and not spread myself thinly to please everyone and end up not enjoying either of them.

As it turned out, this was so the right decision. Because I said no to stopping at 6pm whatever or wherever we were and getting over to my studio, letting the session with Kurupt FM run on for as long as we needed, I felt as though I was in the moment the whole time. I had nowhere else to be; I was fully present and invested and it felt totally right. We were flowing – we hadn't even finished half the song by 6pm – and what we came up with ended up being the song 'Summertime' that was their next single. I felt good. I'd had the conversation with myself. I'd paused, tuned in and decided not to split myself.

Making that decision wasn't easy, but, trust me, when you have a few like that under your belt and you lean further into the pause and start to breathe out – when you say no with compassion and grace – really, the world doesn't stop turning and people don't fall down in a disappointed heap because you have said you can't or would prefer a different way forward. As you grow in confidence, it all makes for a better you and for a better atmosphere for others around you too. No way would Mike have wanted me back at the studio after cutting short the Kurupt FM session that would have inevitably ended before all the good stuff had been completed. I'd have arrived on one level dissatisfied with myself for dipping out, with an unconscious pressure placed on Mike to make up for that during our session.

JUST CHILLIN'

I have a reiki teacher, Mehendra, who helps to balance my energies and allow my body to heal. For so long I'd wanted to find an expert practitioner who understood the alternative ways of harnessing energy to aid in healing, especially my back, so the introduction to him through Emily's boyfriend Sam was really appreciated. I found that reiki worked even better when it was incorporated with grounding exercises, especially meditation. Breathing, stilling yourself and noticing things around you is one of the best ways of tapping into the power of the pause, and one I've come to enjoy. Meditation is a practice I now do for 45 minutes every night before going to sleep. I want to share this with you because it's such a magical experience and has done me so much good. I'd love you to think about it and maybe incorporate it into your life too.

But first, I want to say that mediation comes in all sorts of forms and doesn't have to involve sitting in a Buddha-like position with your legs crossed and your hands in your lap. You can go for a 20-minute walk around the block or through your local park to get some fresh air and clear your mind.

Even walking back from the chippy, eating salt-and-vinegar-drenched chips, can calm your mind.

The evenings suit me well because the calmness I get from being still sets me up for a good night's sleep. Whatever time of day works for you is good. Whenever you choose to mediate, one pro tip that I have is to make sure your stomach isn't too full, so go easy on the size of that portion of chips. You don't want to feel heavy and bloated; you want to feel as light as you can.

At around 9.15pm, I go upstairs and take a nice warm shower. I'm aware of thoughts dropping in, but, after a couple of moments, the water's flowing and I'm not really thinking about anything. When I'm comfortable and have had enough, I turn on the cold water, quick and icy to fire me back up a bit – you don't want to fall asleep during meditation – and then, as I am drying myself, I open my bedroom window a bit, spray the room with some rose water, light up my positive vibe incense sticks and a couple of candles and get into my trackies. When I feel the atmosphere is calm and flowing, I set my alarm for 45 minutes; put my phone on silent, dim it, place it by my bed, on the other side of the room to where I'm going to meditate, and turn off any overhead or side lights.

Then I get comfortable. I like to sit upright on a comfy chair I have in my bedroom, my back against cushions. By now, the smell of the incense is beautiful and the flickering of the candle soothing, and I start to go into the zone. Closing my eyes, I put in some earplugs so it's super quiet with no excess noise. You might like to listen to music, but, for me, I like to close down some of my other senses to access my inner self.

And then I can hear my heart beating, the sound of my blood running through me, and I take a deep breath in, holding it and then breathing out for five, four, three, two, one. I do this three times, keeping my eyes open, making sure the air goes all the way down, and then, the third time, I try to breathe up from my feet. This centres me into my body. I close my eyes and so my meditation begins.

In the first five minutes I find that I'm still aware of my surroundings and my mind is active. *Are the cushions behind my back going to fall; are my trackies comfortable?* I'm fidgeting and moving, my hands are getting into what feels like a spiritual position and then they reach for my rose quartz crystal and all of me acts a bit more spiritual. At the same time, I can't help thoughts from the day wandering in and out of my mind, until I get to a moment, usually about 15 minutes in, when I'm calm, able now to hold my space.

By this time, I know I'm not thinking any more. My breathing is deep and natural. My eyes are closed. Behind them it's kind of all black with not much going on. But within a few seconds, for me, the patterns and shapes begin, then a kaleidoscope of colours starts to appear. I allow the colours to flow, I hear this sort of ringing, a vibration, like an octave of notes. I have hit that sweet spot and I am meditating.

There's no profound moment that prompts me to 'come back' again and it's only when I hear my phone alarm that I open my eyes, stretch, blow out the candles and get straight into bed. I'm out for the count within a few moments, into a deep and peaceful sleep – my golden ticket to the magical world of dreams and so different to the agony and insomnia I experienced during my darkest days.

Having adopted this new way of life, being fully present in whatever I do, taking the time to pause and slow down, I've found that I'm more receptive to the hypnotic vibes all around me; I'm in sync with life rather than trying to resist the beauty it has to offer or trying to box it up. And freeing myself to go on into the night also resulted in 'Maybe', a song on my latest album *22* which I wrote at 3am with Mike playing acoustic guitar. And that song was written after an amazing session with rapper Wretch 32, during which we created another song, 'What More Could I Ask For?', that's on the album too. I felt so creatively inspired, that the *next* day, I composed 'Teardrops', way after what would have been my 8pm cut-off. Each time I hear those songs, I think about how they might never have been written if I hadn't paused to think about how I needed to switch up my studio time.

The way my plants have taught me to stay present is amazing, as are those moments when I get magical downloads of creativity and answers to questions that I may have written down earlier in the day while I'm tending to them. In the pause, I hear everything. Now I've got so much music in me. And my takeaway from all this is that, from little seeds – like the lemons that I planted back in March 2020 – mighty big dreams can grow. Try it.

In the pause,
I hear everything.

CHAPTER THIRTEEN
My Heart's Been Waiting

One Sunday morning during the second coronavirus lockdown, I woke up with Maria Carey's 1995 classic 'Always Be My Baby' in my head. It was such a joyful feeling, being reconnected to that time and place when she first released that track; when my creativity was flowing and I was so in tune with my life.

I was in my white fluffy bathrobe and my hair was mashed up, but I wanted to stay there, in the pause – with nothing in my mind but the song. I started to sing along with her honey-warm voice and felt like filming a bit, in the moment, and put it on my Instagram, writing that good music is 'medicine for the soul'. It turned out that loads of people loved it and sent it on to their friends. That was satisfaction enough for me, so imagine when, a few hours later, Mariah herself posted the clip on her Insta writing, 'Love this so much! Thank you Craig.'

Perhaps it's a surprise to you that this meant so much to me. But it did, because it linked me back to my past. In the moments when we feel disconnected from our more innocent, uninhibited selves, I believe it's important to try to connect with the child in you – the part of you that may have been repressed or not listened to for a while. Life isn't meant to be serious 24/7; as much as there are times when we need to focus on things that require a great deal of our attention, life can also be playful and joyful. For that to happen, we need to stay connected to our childhood selves. There have been other times, when things might have felt a bit funky, a little too much, when I have been able to tune into the feeling I got when I remember the smile on my nan's face, and the anticipation in my tummy, as I tucked into her magical stew; or when I was pressing 'Print' on a freshly designed mixtape cover; or the times when I walked home from a session in the studio with the Artful Dodger, 'Rewind' blasting through my headphones. When I can connect back to those moments, I feel a touch lighter, a touch more playful, a touch like the old (young) me.

Some time ago, an accountant came to see me at home. He was dressed very formally and seemed a touch ill at ease. I wasn't sure if that's because we were meeting for the first time, or because he was uncomfortable in what he was wearing or the day just wasn't going well for him. We sat across from each other at the kitchen table and he started laying out what we were going to be covering. And as I looked over at him, his face so serious, his manner so tense, I decided to do something to change the vibe. I got up from the table and went next door to my living room. I picked up a gigantic bowl full of those colourful Lindor balls of creamy, delicious chocolate, carried it back to where he was sitting and put it down in front of him. I said, 'Help yourself. Take as many as you like. These are all for you.'

If you could have been there, seeing how he turned from being stunned at the size of the mound of chocolates to his face breaking into this huge, playful smile, you would know what I mean when I tell you that he was back in touch with his childhood self. All those chocolates and all for him. What child never dreamed of that happening? He looked from the chocolates to me and laughed with sheer, innocent pleasure. And rather than telling me that he couldn't possibly; he had to think of his weight; he couldn't eat while working, he plunged his hands into the bowl of chocolates and took out one of each colour. As he unwrapped the first one and ate it, unwrapped the second one and ate it, we started chatting and vibing. He got through some more and life felt good. I saw the real him for a moment, before he reverted back to being 'Mr Accountant'.

Ad-libbing over that Mariah track gave me this same feeling of connection to the old me and also got me thinking about where I was now. This period coincided with the 20th anniversary of *Born To Do It*. I wanted to do something to celebrate but, as touring live wasn't possible because of the coronavirus pandemic, I decided to do a global live concert instead. Performing the whole album in full was really special for me, and the icing on the cake was inviting the garage legend DJ Spoony to do a set. Spoony has always supported me from day one and this was such a powerful, full-circle moment, an echo of those early days when I was working the clubs as DJ Fade.

When I stopped to really think about how far I'd come, it made me realise that I *had* done something here. My new music was connecting just like it had 20 years before and my first-ever album was still relevant, being streamed to a whole new generation, and I was part of my fans' lives. I wasn't an imposter. It was me who had written and recorded those songs; it was me who had given people joy as they danced or, as many have told me, got married or gave birth listening to my songs. I recognised that my music *was* sustaining and had meaning and was out there still bringing good vibes to people.

And there were the facts of it too –*Born To Do It* has sold over 7 million copies and a few days previously I'd received a plaque for a billion streams from my last two albums. And finally the penny dropped. This was no fluke. I *had* been given this gift to write songs, to make people happy, and I *do* have something to bring through.

BRAND NEW

My life has been a journey of connecting, disconnecting and reconnecting; to music, to people, to myself. Since I found my singing voice, all I've ever wanted to do is to connect with people. And if I have done that and can continue to do that – through my music, through the discoveries I have made, and now through sharing my innermost thoughts with you – then I'm happy. Connecting is how friendships blossom, how love grows, how we support each other through good times and bad.

We need more connection, more conversation, more sharing. Everyone goes through bad days and bad periods in their life, but by talking about them more with our friends or family or offering a listening ear, it's then that we understand that we share so many of the same experiences and aren't in this alone – that, together, we're stronger. For me, as a man, this is about connecting more to sensitivity, to the feminine energy in us as well as the masculine. I'd love for more men to know that it's OK to connect, to share, to unburden, to express ourselves.

Recently I spoke to Steven Bartlett on his podcast, 'The Diary of a CEO', about this, and to see how it chimed with so many listeners was moving. In interviewing me, Steven took me to a place that I've not always felt comfortable sharing on a public platform, but the connection we made personally was not only empowering, but a beautiful life-affirming moment. Others, such as Jay Shetty, Lewis Howes, Dr Joe Dispenza, Phil Good and Pedro Dos Santos, are also doing great things by holding space for men to express themselves and break down the traditional concepts of masculinity.

Through connection comes a greater understanding – of ourselves and of others. If we take a moment to tune in, then we can be more compassionate and we can be kinder. For me, kindness is humanity's greatest asset. Kindness is grace. It requires strength and, in being kind, we get a sense of well-being like no other.

And there is no greater kindness than self-compassion – being gentle, kind and understanding towards ourselves. Maybe you know the feeling that, however many times someone tells you something about yourself – 'you're looking good', 'you're such a great person' – unless you believe it in the depths of your soul, the words can sound hollow. Now, don't get me wrong – others' approval held weight for me, as you know, as all I ever wanted to do was please other people. But I'm finally able to give *myself* that approval. Realising this was a *gigantic* step for me. Sometimes, with the longer view, these revelations come to us.

And it's not that I suddenly woke up and thought: *I'm the best* or that I wanted to shout it from the rooftops. I've been there before, where being Number One, having the bestselling album, the most streams, the most hits, meant I was riding the crest of the wave, up there at the top. But being at the top isn't sustainable, and I know from past experience that you can come crashing down without a life jacket. I've learned from that and the feeling I have now is such a quiet, internal thing, that it is a bit like this layer of peace has settled into my heart. You can have the ups and you can have the downs and be better and stronger for them, but holding the middle ground, as I've discovered, is definitely a good place to be.

NO HOLDING BACK

Just like in Justin Bieber's hit song 'Love Your Self', it's only when we realise that it's actually healthy to pour love into our own cup first that we see how much more can overflow to others from this place. Rather than trying to give from a cup half empty, it's when we are full of love that we can give even more. For me, this means that you have come to know your-self through some element of soul-searching, asking yourself questions and acting on the answers best for you.

I've been friends with Fearne Cotton ever since she came to Miami to interview me in 2010. We'd hung out a bit both there and in London, and we'd discovered this soul-to-soul connection, which I'm happy to say continues to this day. When she invited me to her wedding in July 2014, at first I was conflicted about going, as over the past few years she'd been appearing on *Celebrity Juice* with Leigh Francis, which was a confusing one for me in terms of our friendship.

While, of course, I wanted to celebrate with Fearne and her fiancé Jesse and accepted their invitation, I was also anxious about being in the same room as the man who had caused my life to implode. And once the media cottoned on (no pun intended) that we were both going to be in the same place at the same time, they ramped it up big time. Going into the reception after the ceremony, I felt this heaviness weighing on me, the pressure mounting.

As much as I'd played things out in my mind beforehand, nothing prepared me for the intensity of actually seeing him at the reception, especially as, once other guests had clocked us on opposite sides of the room, there was this mighty air of anticipation at what might happen. Whether I liked it or not, after all these *Bo' Selecta!* years, things were coming to a head, one way or another.

To this day, I am not sure what happened in the few seconds it took between seeing him and something crystallising in the very, very deepest part of me. But, just like that moment in my car in Miami when my life flashed before my eyes, I suddenly felt the pain of the kid who had endured Johnny's bullying, the pain of the racism that my dad had faced and the pain that I'd had to live with being relentlessly bullied by a guy wearing a black-faced rubber mask, all rise up inside of me simultaneously. And, in that moment, I knew that I could no longer continue to play the slave to this cruel storyline and this was my chance to unshackle myself from the power Leigh Francis's horrible caricature had had over me.

This moment became the moment in which I reclaimed my self-love in the face of all the pain he had caused me and my loved ones. And as I glanced over at Fearne and Jesse, so happy in their love and newly-made vows, I knew I was in a safe place, a happy place, so I harnessed all my internal courage and all the pride I had in who I was and where I had come from, and walked towards him.

The words we exchanged, and the awkward embrace that was later reported in the media, are a blur to me now, but what remains clear is that I no longer feel the sadness I had felt for all those years. I have no idea to this day if Leigh Francis truly feels accountable for the damage he caused me and the others he parodied. But I do know that by realising that I could reach in and claim self-love, even in this most difficult of encounters, was momentous for me and I left that wedding a great deal happier than when I'd walked in.

LOVE WILL COME AROUND

It's taken a while, but I've realised that the time has come to deal with the life experiences of those formative teen years that threw my private life off course, particularly when it comes to finding love. If you were to hurt your ankle, for a while you wouldn't be able to walk on that foot, but, after a while, even though instinctively you might be scared of the pain and you'd limp a bit, you would eventually walk again. What's the difference between that and opening myself up to love?

A lot of the thoughts in this book have come to me while I've been in my garden. The power of nature is *real*. Those vibes are *real*. Tending those plants and flowers has also helped me focus my thoughts about love and relationships – on the importance of caring.

Before I started gardening, I would only buy cut flowers. They'd look amazing and, for a few days, I'd get so much pleasure from their beauty. But when the water went funky and started to smell and the flowers died, that was the end. I'd buy replacements and start all over again.

When I got into gardening, I was introduced to the joy of plants that evolve and change through the seasons. No perfectly cut bouquet that dazzles and delights on immediate impact, but fades just as quickly; with a bit of patience, commitment and understanding, I had flowers blooming from plants and the unexpected joy of knowing that I had helped them, nurtured them to get to that moment. When I started growing orchids and it came to the time when the flowers fell off, at first, instead of leaning into the cycle of regrowth, I'd go and buy new ones in flower, so I could always have them at what I believed to be their best. I didn't trust that they would return and I didn't have the patience to wait. Now, when I'm left with just stems and dead flower heads, it isn't a shock, but more of a knowing that this is how nature works and all that's needed is the right care and attention and the flowers will come back strong and healthy again.

I then discovered over time the joy of 'just green' plants – flowerless plants, like my snake plant. The key to the snake plant, and others like it, is that it's hardy and reliable. At first, I wondered, *Where's the appeal? There aren't any flowers going on.* Then, I started to see, flowers or not, it had this calming, beautiful presence, this reassurance that it was rooted and it was constant and, whatever the time frame, it wasn't going anywhere. It didn't need much watering and it didn't seem to need my undivided attention. It was happy just 'being'.

I have now spent a lot of time with these plants and they have helped me see why my approach to love – yes, love – has been flawed for so many years. For too long, I was impressed by the appearance of someone, drawn towards them through desire, a chemical pull that brought us together, like the beautiful scent of flowers. And that was fun and enjoyable and suited my life at the time. But, looking back, it made me too reliant on short-term gratification. I was not patient enough to weather all the seasons with one person, to get to know them, to invest time nurturing what we had for fear our relationship would not bloom into anything more meaningful and that I would be hurt and disappointed. I was moving too fast, I was a little bit reckless; there were people trying to get to my heart, but I wouldn't stand still for long enough or unlock my emotions to let them in.

Whenever I've got to the point in a relationship where the old pattern of *can't commit because I'll get hurt* meets the longing for something beautiful, new and substantial, I've been conscious of the fight my mind and heart have been having.

If, like me, you've been hurt before, as soon as there's the slightest sign of the heart starting to open up, the mind will instantly kick into action to give you hundreds of reasons as to why you should be careful and why love could be dangerous. But the heart has a whole other plan. The difference with the heart is that it's courageous and wants to dive in. It wants to experience what love could be like, what it will feel like, what the future may hold. And yet the mind doesn't want anything to do with it as anything it can't control is deemed dangerous – its default setting is to protect us from potentially getting hurt all over again.

This is where we meet in this beautiful moment. My advice to you is also directed as much to myself, but I'm ready, and maybe you are too, to lean in and break the cycle. Just like in the bridge of my song with KSI, 'Really Love'.

But what if you've been getting ready for this moment, what if you have a beautiful container of self-love that you've been creating, something already whole, to share? Then, when

Without some measure of self-love, looking to someone else to fulfil your life is dangerous.

you come to a relationship, you are autonomous and confident, as far as you can be, in who you are. You are looking for someone to walk life's course alongside you, two individuals together who can share the magic and romance that life has to offer rather than trying to squeeze every drop of it out of the other person and wondering why things don't last.

No one is going to complete you – and that applies to all relationships in life. Other people can bring things to the table that might make you feel better and happier about your life and yourself, but no one can make you happy if you are not already happy. Without some measure of self-love, looking to someone else to fulfil your life is dangerous.

I can see now – through the floral evidence in front of me – that what will last, what will endure through thick and thin, is a relationship that has roots. The whole Hollywood notion that there is someone out there who will complete you – a half meets another half and then it's a whole – doesn't sit right with me. From my point of view, a more evolved relationship is when two people meet, two fully whole people, and they complement and enhance each other, they are not *dependent* on the other person making them whole or happy. Roots are foundations from which things grow and both people in a romantic relationship need to plant those roots. Sometimes there will be flowers, sometimes there will be just green, but one thing there will always be is continuous growth.

When my sister Amber got married to her lovely partner Sunil in Southampton in the summer of 2021, I was about to feel what those beautiful roots of real love, communion and foundation felt like once again, something that had seemed like a distant memory to me for so long. My sister had been looking forward to this day for some time, especially as the coronavirus lockdown had interrupted her plans, as it did for so many at that time. Prior to the wedding, she had messaged me about possibly creating a specific mix for her to walk down the aisle to – something I was honoured to be asked to be a part of. She wanted K-Ci & JoJo's 'All My Life' mixed into a live version of John Legend's 'You & I (Nobody In The World)'. So I got to work getting the right versions, finessed a mix that was the perfect length and got it over to Amber to send on to the wedding planner to slot into the day's proceedings. At one point while making the mix, I contemplated ringing up the wedding planner and organising a surprise performance for Amber on the day, by having a grand piano rolled out just before she walked out and then singing both of the songs for her to make the occasion even more special. But something that Amber had said to me while I was creating the music resonated with me in a way that made me reconsider.

When I'd finished the final version, after thanking me for making it exactly the way she wanted, she said, 'Craig, I just want you to know how much it means to me that you'll be there for me and Sunil as I know how busy you are. I really want you to enjoy my wedding and not feel like you have to do and be anything else but my brother who I love so much.' It was these words that made me stop in my tracks and abandon the impromptu performance idea; *I did want to be there to enjoy the occasion and I didn't want to have to do anything. I* did *want to simply be her brother watching his sister, who he loves so much, get married.* So with this, I made plans to pick up my mum en route and be fully immersed in the experience – without me overlaying any of my people-pleasing tendencies – at my intuitive sister's request.

The sun was shining as we arrived and made our way to the seated area outside that had been beautifully dressed for the occasion. Part of me had been a little anxious to see so many of my extended family as I felt that it might detract from what we had all come to enjoy – my sister and Sunil finally having their moment, their special day. Thankfully, the vibe was calm and everyone was super respectful of the occasion which made me feel at ease as I took my seat. Sitting among my family and Sunil's beautiful relatives, I could feel the warm air of happiness and love, everyone so connected it was as if I was getting a taste of what was to come in my own life sometime in the future; a feeling I'd never really entertained, but now felt vividly. As the music began, I could feel every note, every lyric touch my soul; it was like I was singing, but also so present in my seat as a guest enjoying the occasion.

Watching my sister walk down the aisle with my dad holding her arm as she cried tears of pure joy and happiness, sent a wave of deep love through me and everyone who witnessed this beautiful joining of two people in love. As Amber reached the altar, I could see Sunil so present, so attentive to her every need and felt overwhelmed with emotion, thankful that my little sister was so happy and had found such a great man in Sunil who would take care of her and love her for the rest of her life. For Amber and Sunil to get to this moment they had both worked on being the best versions of themselves, which, in turn, allowed them to start their married journey from a place of balance and strength, both showing up in their truest form able to live their best lives together. As they exchanged their vows, I could see my dad, who was holding space for them both, shed a tear which, like a chain reaction, made me well up too – I could feel his joy in his beautiful daughter now moving to a new phase of her life and, at the same time, the sadness of him realising that his role had also changed; a gentle letting go and acceptance was simultaneously being experienced.

This was such an unexpected, profound healing experience for me. It not only opened my heart in a way that I hadn't thought possible, but showed me what real love was all about. I was experiencing the love for my sister, for her husband, for my dad and for my mum, and the deep connection to all my family members. In this moment, I felt whole again.

So here I am telling you, I've not been able to let in real love since those fleeting moments with Nicky back in Southampton. It's unbelievable to think how much of an impact a moment like that can have on a 17-year-old kid and how it ultimately affected how I related to others for years after. This is my greatest life lesson of all. You might be holding back from something in your life, perhaps love too, and you might not even realise it – I didn't realise this for many years – but you are missing out, as I have missed out. It's not too late to change that for the better.

What really helped me start to heal the wound was being able to go back to that initial feeling when my heart closed and just sit with it; to go back to that time and remember all the details. This wasn't easy – talk about feeling like I was reliving it all again, but, this time, rather than racing past it and pretending that it was OK and then shoving it down in my subconscious, I was able to bring it into the light, see it clearly for what it was: a moment in my life that hurt like being burned, not a nice feeling, but not something that should have become the precursor for every relationship I would then enter into in my life.

I transported myself back to my small bedroom in Southampton and gave my 17-year-old self with his broken heart a huge hug, telling him: 'It's OK now, I've got you and you don't have to feel this pain anymore.' And, trust me, in that moment, I truly felt a lightness in my heart, as if the padlock had snapped open and the shackles had fallen away.

In healing terms, this is what is known as a 'soul retrieval' – taking back, reclaiming, a piece of our soul that got fragmented when we gave away our power either during a traumatic situation or to a person or circumstance that left us feeling like a piece of us had been lost or taken. By bringing it back home, I was able to heal that part of me – the highest form of self-love.

I can now see how much the moments that were intense and life-affirming became a part of me. The women I've had relationships with have all taught me important lessons, giving me valuable insight into how closed my heart was. I've thought about them and, where possible, I've faced up to the hurt I might have caused, disappointed in myself at the disservice I might have done when all they were trying to do was to get me to open my heart.

I've also recognised that, just like that Artful Dodger classic featuring Romina Johnson 'Movin' Too Fast', rushing into intimacy is not always the best way forward if you want to experience real love. Energy and vibe are far more important than looks. The sexiest thing for me is when someone's got their own confidence. And also when we can laugh together. Laughter is one of my highest values in relationships. If you make me laugh, you've got half my heart already because, for me, that's going to be a saving grace through our intoxicating romantic ups and our less intoxicating romantic downs.

Perhaps you have been hurt or have found it easier to put love aside to focus on your work, your children or finding your way in the world. Perhaps love is missing from your life too. Perhaps reading this will help you come to terms with that and reopen yourself up to the possibility to love. I genuinely believe only good will come of doing this, now other parts of my life are rebalanced.

Watch this space.

Energy and vibe are far more important than looks.

CHAPTER FOURTEEN
Best of Me

For too long I'd been hiding behind my real feelings. When it came to that dark night, my soul broken by the pain in my back, tumbling me into freefall, if I hadn't been able to get to the bottom of what it was, beyond the pain of my back, that was contributing to my mental deterioration, I am not sure I'd still be here today. But having my mum and dad, Colin, Gina and other family and friends to help me, people bearing me in mind and seeing me; having people to work with me on my physical recovery; having Sonia and Belinda to guide me when I found myself disconnected from my spirit, I was seen and I was held and I was able to heal. What I learned is that, for me to function on any level, my well-being is the most important part of my life because, from that place, I am able to regulate life. Having had this acute experience, I now know that maintaining my mental health is no different to maintaining my physical health. Both need tending to, nurturing, caring for and, like my plants, they need to be given the time to weather the storm of life. Some days the sun shines and some days the wind blows us off course, and that's OK.

In the end, my back had my back. From those dark times came the light and my rejuvenation. Having this experience allowed me to tune into my mental and physical state, to disconnect from some of my obsessive and unhealthy patterns of behaviour and to reconnect with the true me, the best me: the me that has leaned into my inner self and my intuition; the me that has learned – is still learning – to say yes only when I mean yes; the me that has discovered how to recognise my boundaries; the me that understands the power of the pause; the me that has learned how to better hold my truth; the me that has unlocked my heart and is ready for love.

I've also – and this is something that I hope you will be able to do too – tuned in, with a healthy dose of introspection, to what I've been afraid of facing or dealing with. In peeling back the layers of my fears to the core to see what needed to be done to heal them, I have made some profound changes to the way in which I live. Without this process, I just knew I would be bypassing any real change for the better and was setting myself up for more of the same.

As the psychoanalyst Carl Jung wrote: 'When the diagnosis is correct the healing begins.' Well, I know that to be true

Some days the sun shines and some days the wind blows us off course, and that's OK.

because, having done some deep soul retrieval, locating the parts of me that had been locked away which were holding me back from the fullness of life, I can now say that I am alive to the joy in life, my creativity flowing, music running through my veins, no longer afraid to confront my demons. I have hit the sweet spot, can speak my truth and share my stories.

While my story is different to yours, some of the ways in which I realigned myself may chime with you. Reframing the way I approached and interacted with positivity has led me to this place today where I'm able to look at things for what they are, no longer having to be the people-pleaser, the guy with the brightest smile, straining those positive vibes.

And to tell you the truth, it's only recently, since I've learned that negativity isn't wrong, scary or something we have to sweep under the carpet – that it's OK to admit harsh truths; that you can lean into them, feel them, pause and take time to honour they exist – that I've come to see that you can create space between the negative feeling and you, and in that space it no longer has its intense grip on you. By drilling down to exactly what it is that is pulling us out of alignment, it can be seen clearly and then healed. Just like a car with the axel out of alignment, however big or small, it's always going to pull left or right until that wonky part is fixed – or, in our case, healed. Only then can we move uninhibited and, with this, we can achieve a better sense of alignment.

By doing this, I have released new feelings and gained new insights into living a healthier and more balanced life in which my mental well-being is as nourished as my physical. I've also learned to be kinder to my body, to respect it, to embrace a healthy lifestyle and push back from the six-pack culture.

RELOAD

I have accepted myself for who I am, no longer seeing myself as an imposter, happy in who and where I am at this point in my life. I have accepted that I need to be vulnerable, that there is power in this, and I can see now that, over the years, I've acted out of self-protection, jumping in to control situations so I couldn't be hurt.

Don't get me wrong, I still have things to learn and places to grow, but in doing some work on understanding myself and changing up aspects of my behaviour and ways of engaging,

I've relinquished the need to control so many parts of my life. I'm free to let life lead the way.

I have recognised that, despite the kickbacks or times in my life when my creativity hasn't flowed so well, my music has remained constant and meaningful. It has certainly been one of my greatest teachers too. It has shown me in a myriad of ways the qualities of real relationships, be it giving time and space to grow, or simply creating a safe environment to be able to be fully expressive, where everything can be laid bare on the table and where vulnerability is truly honoured and embraced. Music has been my most enduring love, my greatest friend.

I would say to any aspiring artist who's putting out music and having some success: enjoy it, be immersed in the here and now, because if you start to look to what will be going on next week, next month, next year, your moment will disappear. It will be over before you know it.

I've learned that the true art of living isn't about constantly reaching for the destination we've set for ourselves, but to enjoy the journey on the way. It's funny that, even when I had achieved most of the dream goals I had set out, it always felt as though they never quite lived up to the expectation nor compared to the thrill I got out of the journey getting to them. I've realised now that by making the journey the actual destination, it doesn't matter so much about where I end up, but is more about enjoying the magic and colour of being fully in the process on the way. With this simple flip, we can enjoy any goals that we achieve, but also aren't left feeling discouraged if we don't. This way, we get to feel alive and present in the adventure of it all.

22

It's been 22 years since *Born To Do It* and my latest album is called *22*. If you've been with me all along, then I am overwhelmed and so grateful that you are still here enjoying this wonderful ride. And if you have recently joined the journey, then welcome.

22. You couldn't make it up. Not the actuality of it – the maths of the 22 years between 2000 and 2022 – but what the number means in the world of numerology and angel numbers, something that is very close to my heart. 22 is a 'Master Builder Number' because it is so resonant. It is a number that symbolises bringing high-level vibes from the spiritual realm and grounding them in the physical here on earth to create a better environment. It's also my angel's way of telling me that I am on the right track and that making soul-to-soul – rather than role-to-role – connections is what I came here to do. 22 is a number that is telling me that my wisdom is enough for me to be in charge of the true me, to trust in myself and be true to myself, to pay attention to my intuition (I told you I couldn't make it up) and to take charge of my own destiny.

Lockdown gave me time to write songs. There was no rush. It felt a lot like when I was writing *Born To Do It*, when I was completely true to myself because there was no weight of expectation on me. I was still a kid at heart then and, for this album, being in my home, writing lyrics, laying down tracks, I felt free again; like I'd returned to the true me. I've got garage on there, I've got R&B and I've got songs that are a beautiful culmination of where I'm at now.

Over these 22 years, I've seen how my music has become not only a time stamp of memories in many people's lives, but has also given them healing, hope and happiness, both when life feels light and when life feels heavy. I was overwhelmed during my 'Hold That Thought' tour in April 2022 (another 22) seeing so many people from all walks of life, a whole variety of ages, up and down and across the country, connected as one. I've got to tell you that the same Notting Hill moment of euphoria re-entered my heart as I heard everyone singing my lyrics and then, igniting as one, dancing and moving to the sounds and rhythms of my TS5 sets.

And when I was invited to do one of these sets at the Platinum Party at the Palace to celebrate the Queen's 70 years of service to our country, I was thrilled to have been chosen alongside some wonderful artists, including Alicia Keys, Nile Rodgers, Diana Ross, Jax Jones, Mabel, Celeste, Sigala and Andrea Bocelli. The day itself was full of good vibes and, on the way to the Palace, I thought about a man

I'd met when I'd gone to Windsor Castle to collect my MBE at the end of 2021, who had organised online viewings for people who hadn't been able to attend the funerals of their loved ones during the pandemic. At first, he'd done this for his friends, but then, as word got around, he was inundated with requests from people in his community and beyond. And out of the beautiful kindness of his heart, he didn't hesitate, dedicating himself to helping those families get through those difficult times by making their load a little lighter. Like the Queen, who does so much behind the scenes, it's what we do when no one is looking that really matters and, on this day of national celebration, I was happy to be able to perform for all the sung and unsung heroes who make such a difference to other people's lives.

On the big day, waiting for my cue at the side of the stage, I noticed, as I paused to centre myself, the huge golden angel at the top of the Queen Victoria Memorial. She was being protected by four archangels and, as the stage manager called out '22 seconds' (you couldn't make that up either), at that moment I knew that the angels had my back. I walked out onto the stage and felt the love, energy and vibes coming from the crowd lining the Mall, waving their red, white and blue flags, and I burst into my first song 'Ain't Giving Up'.

Later, as my mum and I walked into the after-party *inside Buckingham Palace*, she squeezed my hand and said, 'Look where we are – inside the Queen's home.'

We looked at each other and I knew what she was thinking as the name of our council block – 'Queen's House' – flashed into my mind. When my mum saw me smiling away, she laughed.

My heart was full of gratitude for all the love and support she had given me right from the start of my life to this moment and I told her, 'You are my true queen, Mum, and I love you.'

We partied the night away and, when Prince William and the Duchess of Cambridge told me how much they had enjoyed my performance and how Prince George had loved my sparkly blue tracksuit, it topped off a truly magical day.

GOT IT GOOD

As I've become more aware of the way my music affects people, enduring and touching generations of listeners, I've realised that my songs hold a frequency that transcends age, gender and background. While the younger me was wide-eyed and aspirational and hungry for success, these days I can see how the choice of the words I use holds some responsibility. If I'm out there in my own life searching for a new masculinity, a society where men no longer have to 'man up' or 'roll with the punches', then I need to reflect that in what I put out there. The personal and the professional are not two different things for me and I am way more conscious of my lyrics now because they can really impact people.

So what would I now tell my younger self? Well, to do it all again exactly the same because you'll learn; that there's power in vulnerability and courage in speaking up; that through adversity you get strength; and that you will have no idea how music will always hold your hand through the ups and the downs. That you're in for one hell of an amazing ride, but you're going to have to negotiate the highs and the lows and, when it feels like the train is coming off the tracks, just know that it's in those moments that – eventually – the right thing will follow.

And that, just like Charlie, when he puts the everlasting gobstopper back on Willy Wonka's table, if you, too, honour your vibes, you will be tuning into your best life.

ACKNOWLEDGEMENTS

Thank you Gillian Stern, for not only holding the space for me to speak my truth, but for encouraging me to go deeper, knowing that all of the real gold would be found there. I feel through our beautiful friendship, I've been able to tell my story in an even more enriched, articulate and vibrant way. In writing this book, I always wanted to gently and tenderly take my readers by the hand and to hopefully help them in their own lives, and you have enabled me to do that. From the day we met I knew the vibe was special and oh, was I right. You are a beautiful human being, who thinks about people deeply and your care for me is beyond appreciated. I'm so grateful to have you in my life and thank you for being the best editor I could ever have asked for.

Thank you to Julia Kellaway, who made the last stages of preparing the manuscript so much fun. Sharing your own experiences of the stories I was writing about, right back from the Artful Dodger days to now, made it so vibey. We'll always be singing those chapter lyrics, even if they were written in invisible ink.

My heartfelt thanks to my agent Caroline Michel at PFD and to my team at Ebury – Lizzy Gray, Emily Brickell and Laura Higginson. I appreciate you creating the best environment for me to share my story.

Thank you Fearne Cotton, for being so supportive throughout my journey of writing this book. It's such a full-circle moment having it come out through your inspiring Happy Place imprint and I couldn't think of a better place for it to live.

Thank you Sonia Choquette, for the wonderful conversations and insight. You are a blessing in my life and, by showing me how to be more grounded in my body, you have helped me feel my vibes more acutely. Bright Light and Figgy are dancing at the adventure they're on.

Thank you Kenneth Bowser for teaching me the profound impact of the astrological placement of planets. Your readings have enabled me to better navigate the ebb and flow of my life.

Thank you Carly, for bringing your good vibes wherever I am. You have no idea how your presence can shift the whole energy of a room for the better when you walk in. Your care and love is so appreciated.

Thank you Jack, for working so hard to deliver my ideas and creations to the world. Trust me, I know it's not easy, with me always pushing for perfection. I'm eternally appreciative and grateful for you, and your calm, caring, efficiency. We'll have to do that celebration Part 2, minus the early exit and guitar playing, for your next birthday. And Emily, you and Sam will have to come too. I'm so happy that your then new boyfriend is now part of the family. Watching you and Jack both grow into the beautiful human beings you are, makes my heart smile.

Thank you Gina, for all the warm salted cashews baked with love, that fuelled me as I wrote this book. Your love and care, while I poured my self in to this new adventure was the perfect balance I needed. Reminding me to get some sleep, when you knew I was lost in the writing, always preparing the best food, when I'd forget to eat, and always going above and beyond to make everything calm and organised in my home. You're an angel in my life, and no matter what I have going on in my head, you always find a way to remind me to pause and come back to the beautiful moment. Plus, no one makes me cry with laughter like you.

As always, my thanks and love to Colin, my best friend, soul mate and manager. Our journey is something, so divinely orchestrated, that all I can do is smile at the serendipity of it all. Growing into a man with you by my side has been the most enriching experience I could ever have wished for. Your grace and openness to allow me to share some of our more difficult conversations in the book, is exactly what makes our beautiful relationship so real. You and Amanda accepted me into your family from the beginning and you always protected me like one of your children, and knowing I have a place at your dinner table every Friday night is something I cherish. My life is so much better for having you in it.

Thank you Amber, for your love and for showing me how to connect with the thing that truly matters, family. I'm so glad that I now have the chance to grow with you and Sunil as we enjoy and make beautiful memories together. Thank you too, to my Aunty Elaine, my Godmother Alison and her beautiful sister, Janette for always believing in me and making time back in Southampton so much fun.

Thank you Dad, for helping me understand from an early age that by doing the right thing, the right thing shall follow. You've always protected me and made sure that I had the support to follow my dreams. Those trips to Paultons Park and days with Nannie over at the house, I carry close to my heart and always will. I'm so proud of the Ebony Rockers mural that was painted in the band's honour in Southampton earlier in 2022, as it not only recognises the music you made, but also your courage and integrity at standing up and speaking out against the injustices so many were facing. The way you always show up to help anyone in need and always speak your truth has been the foundation for me.

And thank you, Mum. For always being there for me and raising me with your unconditional and pure love. The way that you sacrificed your time and resources to provide for me is something that I'll always be eternally grateful for. You set me up for success, just by letting me know that I was enough and you made me feel seen, heard and loved and that is all I could ever ask for. To this day, you shower me in the most thoughtful, beautiful, kind moments of affection and are still my Number One supporter. This book is my way of saying thank you for being my everything and I love you more than you can imagine.

Thank you to all the artists and songwriters who have collaborated with me along the way. You sharing your gifts with me has been more than an honour. To see an idea come to fruition and touch so many people around the world is what we all wish for, and all of you have played a part in realising this dream. Mark Hill, Fraser T Smith, Tre Jean-Marie, Mike Brainchild and all the producers who've helped me in my life, I thank you from the bottom of my heart. Thank you to my band – Kwame Yeboah, Marshall, Adam 'Smiley' Wade, Marcus Mcneish, Shean Williams and Laura V – who always bring the vibe and make performing on stage such a joy. And thank you to my on–the–road team – Mark Friend, Joe McGough, Ash Wilkinson, Pete Whitelaw and Stuart Hunter – for always having my back no matter where I go. All of you are here with me in this book and your energy is in these pages.

Thank you to all my friends and family. There are too many of you to list and I'd need another book to get everyone's name down. You know who you are. I want you all to know how much I appreciate you and how you've all played a part in my journey of becoming the man I am today. You've helped me tune into my vibes, mirror back parts of me that needed healing and showed me how truly precious this life really is.

What an adventure. To be continued …

CREDITS

The following song and album titles have been quoted in this book:

Born to Do It: Can't Be Messing Around (Craig David), Last Night (David/Mark Hill), Walking Away (David/Hill), Time to Party (David/Hill/Jimmy Seals), Once in a Lifetime (David/Hill), You Know What (David/Hill), Rewind (David/Tony Briscoe/Hill), Key to My Heart (David/Jeremy Paul)

Slicker Than Your Average: Slicker Than Your Average (David/Trevor Henry/Anthony Marshall), Fast Cars (David/Henry/Marshall), Hidden Agenda (David/Hill), Rise & Fall (David/Dominic Miller/Gordon 'Sting' Sumner), Personal (David/Henry/Marshall), What's Changed? (David/Hill)

The Story Goes ... : Just Chillin' (David/Rick Nowels), Thief in the Night (David), My Love Don't Stop (David/Antonio Dixon/Harvey Mason, Jr/Eric Dawkins/Damon Thomas)

Trust Me: Awkward (David/Martin Jonsson/Glen Scott/Tommy Sims/Martin Terefe)

Signed Sealed Delivered: All Alone Tonight (Stop, Look, Listen) (David, Abbott Black, Thom Bell, Linda Creed)

Following My Intuition: Ain't Giving Up (David/Bruce Fielder), When the Bassline Drops (David/Tyrone Lindo/Scott Wild), Nothing Like This (David/Adam Englefield/Jacob Manson), Got It Good (David/Jamie Alem/Louis Kevin Celestin/Tre Jean-Marie/Lauren Faith), Louder Than Words (David/Michael Hannides/Alan Sampson), No Holding Back (David/Robbert van de Corput), Here With Me (David/Jean-Marie/Ebenezer Fabiyi), Sink or Swim (David/Celestin/Faith/Jean-Marie)

The Time Is Now: Magic (David/Jean-Marie/Ed Drewett), Heartline (David/Guy James Robin/Sam Romans), Brand New (David/Steve McCutcheon), Love Will Come Around (David/Dixon/Fraser Thorneycroft-Smith/Paul), Somebody Like Me (David/Ché Grant/Manson), Focus (David/Furner/Paul/Thorneycroft-Smith), Reload (David/Will Kennard/Saul Milton), Talk To Me (David/Jean-Marie/Talay Riley)

When You Know What Love Is: When You Know What Love Is (David/Gary Barlow/Thorneycroft-Smith/Janee Bennett)

22: Teardrops (David/Negin Djafari/Michael Engmann/Tim Kelley/Jonathan Buck/Bob Robinson), Who You Are (David/ Uzoechi Osisioma Emenike/Nick Gale/Matt Zara/Joel Hailey/ Rory Bennett), Back to Basics (David/Grace Barker/Thomas Mackenzie Bell/Adrian McLeod), My Heart's Been Waiting for You (David/Djafari/Engmann/Allen George/Fred McFarlane), What More Could I Ask For? (David/Jermaine Scott/Engmann), Obvious (David/Engmann/Priscilla Hairston/Sean Wander), Best of Me (David/Helen 'Carmen Reece' Culver/Engmann/ Mariah Carey/Shawn C Carter/Shirley Elliston/Lincoln Chase/ Narada Michael Walden/Jeffrey E Cohen), Meant to Be (David/ Engmann), Already Know (David/Engmann/Kyle Harvey), Yes (Culver/G'harah 'PK' Degeddingseze)